THE VIRGINAL CONCEPTION
AND BODILY RESURRECTION OF JESUS

The Virginal Conception and Bodily Resurrection of Jesus

by

Raymond E. Brown, S.S.

PAULIST PRESS
New York / Paramus / Toronto

NIHIL OBSTAT
Myles M. Bourke, S.T.D., S.S.L.
Censor Librorum

IMPRIMATUR
✠ James P. Mahoney, D.D.
Vicar General, Archdiocese of New York

January 11, 1973

Library of Congress
Catalog Card Number: 72-97399

ISBN 0-8091-1768-1

Published by Paulist Press
Editorial Office: 1865 Broadway, N.Y., N.Y. 10023
Business Office: 400 Sette Drive, Paramus, N.J. 07652

Printed and bound in the
United States of America

CONTENTS

INTRODUCTION

This book treats two complex and sensitive issues. Studies of the historical Jesus are already complicated today by our realization that the Gospel accounts of the ministry are not simple reporting but developed reflections on the significance of Jesus. However, a study of the conception and resurrection of Jesus is doubly complicated by the fact that these two events lie outside the public domain in which the general ministry of Jesus was set. From the baptism to the crucifixion what Jesus proclaimed by deed and word could be seen and heard by the residents of Galilee and Judea—through Jesus God was acting in the course of history. But a virginal conception could be personally attested only by Mary. No one in the New Testament claims to have seen the resurrection of Jesus, and only believers claim to have seen the risen Jesus. A conception without a human father and a bodily resurrection from the dead imply unique divine interventions from outside the flow of history. They are events that belong to the eschatological period, to that moment when the limits of history yield to God's freedom from space and time.

If the complexities of the two issues affect all Christians, the sensitivities are felt particularly by those Christians concerned with the exactitude of the Gospel accounts and/or with the reliability of Church doctrine. As a Roman Catholic I am aware that vital interest in my own church will be centered particularly on the latter point, since Catholic teaching has not envisioned any alternative to a literal adherence to the virginal conception and the bodily resurrection. But I am also aware that for many Protestants as well as for many Catholics the literal historicity of the biblical accounts of the conception and

1

the resurrection of Jesus is a vital issue. Some of this sensitivity is really fundamentalist in tendency; it presupposes a complete identification of divine truth with past formulations of that truth in Scripture and/or in doctrine, as if the formulations were not substantially affected by the historical limitations of the men who formulated them. But much of the truly conservative sensitivity is not fundamentalist: it recognizes the limitations of past (and of all) formulations of truth; but it insists that despite the limitations there was a grasp of truth in those formulations. This valid conservatism fears that a change in the formulation or in the understanding of the formulation may result in a loss of the insight into truth.

In writing this book I have sought to speak to both the complexities and the sensitivities. While I try to show how critical biblical scholarship would nuance our approach to the Gospel accounts, I seek to do this with enough explanation so that the reader who is open to conviction may see that a *truly* conservative attitude (as opposed to a fundamentalist attitude) need not be affronted by modern approaches to the Bible and to theology.

A short book normally does not need an introduction of any length. But precisely because I am trying to meet sensitivities, as well as complexities, I wish to offer the reader a preliminary explanation of two points: first, why two such diverse topics have peculiar theological significance for Scriptural and theological studies today, especially in the development of Roman Catholic theology; and second, what suppositions about biblical criticism underlie the treatment.

(A) The Theological Significance
of the Two Topics

As I have lectured throughout the United States and abroad to clergy, religious, and laity who are interested in the Bible, I have been struck with how often I am questioned about modern views concerning the virginal conception and the bodily resurrection of Jesus. Obviously the questioners have heard rumors about "new ideas" on these subjects and want to get the biblical facts straight—a refreshing contrast to those whose immediate reaction to rumors of new ideas is one of suspicion or condemnation. Nevertheless, I have asked myself why the peculiar fascination for these two topics when most often the lectures given by me have touched on neither. I now suspect that this interest is implicitly indicative of our having come to a new stage in the development of the Catholic biblical movement in the twentieth century.

A short explanation of what I mean may be useful so that the context and significance of a discussion of the virginal conception and the bodily resurrection are not lost. As a prelude let me guess that history will divide this century roughly into thirds as regards significant movements in the Catholic study of the Bible. The first period (1900-1940) was dominated by the rejection of modern biblical criticism, an attitude forced on the Church by the Modernist heresy. The second period (1940-1970) involved the introduction of biblical criticism by order of Pope Pius XII and the gradual but reluctant acceptance of that criticism by the mainstream of Church thought. The third period (1970-2000), if I guess right, will involve the painful assimilation of the implications of biblical criticism for Catholic doctrine, theology, and practice.

We need not belabor the first period of the Modernist crisis and its aftermath, from 1900 to 1940. It was a time of dangerous heresy, and the saintly Pius X was more interested in protecting the faithful than in the niceties of scientific attitude. In Scripture the Modernists were using the new biblical criticism inaugurated by the German Protestants; and in *Pascendi* and *Lamentabili,* the official Roman condemnations of Modernism, little distinction was made between the possible intrinsic validity of biblical criticism and the theological misuse of it by the Modernists. Between 1905 and 1915 the Pontifical Biblical Commission in Rome issued a series of decisions on many questions of biblical interpretation and authorship. While these decisions were conservative in tone and ran against the trends of biblical criticism, they were often phrased with nuance. But since scholars were obliged to assent, such actions gave to the non-Catholic world the image of a monolithically fundamentalist Catholic attitude toward the Bible—an attitude where questions were not discussed by exchanging scientific opinion but were solved by unquestionable centralized authority. The vigorous ecclesiastical action taken in the 1920's against Catholic biblical scholars who deviated from these directives only reinforced the image.

In the second period (1940-1970) the pontificate of Pius XII marked a complete about-face in attitude and inaugurated the greatest renewal of interest in the Bible that the Roman Catholic Church has ever seen. His encyclical *Divino Afflante Spiritu* (1943) instructed Catholic scholars to use the methods of scientific biblical criticism that had hitherto been forbidden them. It took a little over ten years for teachers to be trained in the new approaches and for their ideas to filter into Catholic seminaries and colleges, so that the mid-1950's really marked the watershed. By that time the critical method had led to Catholic exegetes abandoning almost all the biblical positions taken by Rome at the beginning of the century. This was tacitly acknowledged in 1955 by the secretary of the Pontifical Biblical Commission who stated that Catholic scholars now had complete freedom with regard to the earlier decrees of 1905-1915, except where they touched on faith or morals (and very few of them did).[1] Obviously this turn-about was not without

---

[1] The text of his statement may be found in the *Catholic Biblical Quarterly* 18 (1956), 23-29. Attacks from the ultra-right on modern Catholic biblical studies continue to judge these studies in light of the anti-Modernist decrees. The fatal flaw in such attacks is the failure to recognize that the import of the anti-Modernist decrees is limited by the historical context in which they were written. Since a failure to appreciate historical limitation is intrinsic in the whole ultra-right or fundamentalist position, there is little purpose in attempting to refute such attacks. Nevertheless, it is lucidly clear (and not a matter of theological opinion) that the secretary's statement frees Catholics from any obligation of adherence to those early Biblical Commission decrees in questions of authorship, date, historicity, etc. Fundamentalist Catholics may continue to promote the biblical views of 1905-1915, but they have no right to pass judgment on other Catholics who refuse to do so.

opposition and anguish. In particular, clergy and religious (and thus many of the teachers of the people) were appalled at hearing a new generation mouthing the very ideas they had been taught to consider as wrong and even heretical. Now it was permissible to think that the early stories of Genesis were not historical; that Isaiah was not one book; that Matthew was not the first Gospel and was not written by an apostolic eyewitness; that the Gospels were not four harmonious biographies and were sometimes inaccurate in detail. Nevertheless, once the initial shock of unlearning was over and the positive insights of the new biblical movement were grasped, the mainstream of Catholic thought came to tolerate and, increasingly, to accept with joy the "new" biblical ideas. An attempt to set back the clock after the death of Pius XII and in the first session of the Second Vatican Council was beaten back; and the final form of the Constitution on Revelation (*Dei Verbum,* 1965) gave the Council's stamp of approval to the direction inaugurated by Pius XII.[2]

Thus somewhere in the years just before and after 1970 we have come to the end of this era which I have called the second period of the century—the period of the acceptance of biblical criticism. On the American Catholic scene one might describe the *The Jerome Biblical Commentary* (1968) as a visible monument to the victory in the great biblical battle; for here, twenty-five years after Pius XII's encyclical, was a compendium of critical study written entirely by Catholic scholars who represented almost every major Catholic university, seminary, and theology school in the United States and Canada.[3] On the ecclesiastical scene a landmark might be seen in Pope Paul's action of June 1972 in appointing a new Pontifical Biblical Commission consisting not of cardinals but of twenty schol-

---

[2] For a detailed account of the ecclesiastical difficulties encountered by the Catholic biblical movement between 1958 and 1963 see *The Jerome Biblical Commentary* (Englewood Cliffs: Prentice Hall, 1968), art. 72 §§ 7-8.

[3] It is noteworthy that translations are appearing in Spanish and Italian—the American project has met an international Catholic need.

ars, all of them men committed to the biblical criticism adopted by Pius XII, and some of them (e.g., David Stanley and Stanislaus Lyonnet) men who suffered greatly in the abortive fundamentalist attempts around 1960 to reject that criticism.

If we have reached the stage of an acceptance of the factual results of modern biblical criticism, the skirmishes are not over and so the third period into which we are now entering may yet be troubled. There is always the massive problem of how to disseminate these results in the parish pulpit and in classroom catechetics, not by any harmful techniques of shock, but by way of positive formation of attitudes toward the Bible. But I leave that task to others more skilled in the communication media; and I concern myself here with the problem of the 1970's (and the following years) toward which this book is directed, namely, the impact of the results of biblical criticism on Catholic doctrine and theology.

Now, some who were opposed to this acceptance of biblical criticism within Catholicism found reassurance in face of an apparent defeat by contending that whatever this new breed of Scripture scholar might say about the Bible, the really important factor was the post-biblical Church dogma. In their outlook, modern scriptural investigations could illuminate (or, more likely, obscure) the biblical period that was preparatory for the Church's decision; but that decision, once reached, was immutable, whether it represented the theology of the 4th, or the 16th, or the 19th centuries. They conceived of the exchange between Scripture and tradition as proceeding on a one-way street: tradition could always correct Scriptural interpretation, but never vice versa. If the biblical scholar was going to insist on the freedom to play with his new-fangled toys of language and literary form, he was to be kept in a playpen and not let out to disturb the good order of the theological household.

But here too the implications of Vatican II have upset this nicely ordered domesticity; for the statements of the Council raised biblical exegesis from the status of second-class Catholic citizenship to which it had been reduced by an over-reaction to the Protestant claim for its autonomy. In the Constitution on Divine Revelation (*Dei Verbum,* vi 21) the Fathers of the

Council dared to compare the veneration the Church has for the Scriptures to the veneration it has for the eucharistic body of the Lord. The Council professed that: "Sacred theology rests on the written word of God, together with sacred tradition, as its primary and perpetual foundation" (vi 24). Thus, the relation seems to be that of equality rather than of one-sided primacy of tradition over Scripture: "Sacred tradition and sacred Scripture are to be accepted and venerated with the same sense of devotion and reverence" (ii 9). The living teaching office of the Church "is not above the word of God but serves it" and must listen to the word[4] devoutly as part of the process of interpreting it (ii 10). The model is not one of autonomy, either of tradition over scriptural interpretation (the popular Catholic model of post-reformation times) or of scriptural interpretation over Church tradition (a popular understanding of the Protestant position); the model is one of mutual influence. And this mutual influence will involve tension when one serves to modify the other in promoting the Church's grasp of God's truth.

That the Church's grasp of truth changes and develops is another insight that has become respectable in the aftermath of Vatican II. In the speech with which he opened the Council (Oct. 11, 1962) Pope John XXIII made one of the most important magisterial admissions of recent times: "The substance of the ancient doctrine of the deposit of faith is one thing, and the way in which it is presented is another." The key to the biblical reform described above was the recognition that, while the Scriptures are the word of God, they do not escape the limitations of history. The Scriptures reflect the limited views current in specific periods of human history, and this historical context must be taken into account in interpreting the weight and import of their inspired message. But very often in the Catholic mind the statements of the Church were not seen to be under a similar historical limitation. Yet here was Pope John distinguishing between God's truth and its human formu-

---

[4] "Word of God" is not simply the word of the Scriptures but certainly includes the Scriptures.

lations. Continuing in this same direction, theologians now affirm very clearly that doctrinal formulations capture an aspect of the revealed truth but do not exhaust it. True as they are, formulations represent the limited insight of one period of Church history which can be modified in another period as Christians approach the truth from a different direction or with new tools of investigation.

It will be noted that I said "modified," for I do not think that past insights are wiped out by subsequent developments. A truly Christian sense of tradition limits the possibilities of change. Very often the modification consists in bringing the Church to distinguish between elements of previous formulations that are permanently helpful and elements so time-conditioned that they can best be dispensed with. In other words, the recognition of historical relativity in doctrinal formulations does not constitute a rejection of infallibility,[5] but sharpens our understanding of the range of infallibility so that we seek to delineate more precisely the extent to which the Church has spoken infallibly. The struggle of modern Catholic theology to give precision to the limits of infallibility is not unlike the recent struggle of Catholic biblical studies with the concept of scriptural inerrancy. In the last one hundred years we have moved from an understanding wherein inspiration guaranteed that the Bible was totally inerrant to an understanding wherein inerrancy

---

[5] Some Catholic theologians do reject infallibility, as I shall mention below in discussing the virginal conception (see n. 45); others have emphasized how long it was before Catholics developed the claim to infallibility as we now know it (Brian Tierney, *Origins of Papal Infallibility 1150-1350* [Leiden: Brill, 1972]). Similarly there would be disagreement among Catholic biblical scholars on the value of scriptural formulations. While, as I have indicated, I take a nuanced view in which these formulations do not escape the limitations of history, I would be much more positive about their value than is R. J. Dillon, "Biblical Approaches to the Priesthood," *Worship* 46 (1972) 456-57, who maintains that there can be no direct adoption of a biblical statement as a doctrinal principle. It is one thing to maintain that the biblical statement does not exhaust the truth, but I find Dillon ambiguous as to whether the statement ever captures any permanent truth.

is limited to the Bible's teaching of "that truth which God wanted put into the sacred writings for the sake of our salvation."[6] In this long journey of thought the concept of inerrancy was not rejected but was seriously modified to fit the evidence of biblical criticism which showed that the Bible was not inerrant in questions of science, of history, and even of time-conditioned religious beliefs. Historical and critical studies of doctrine may lead to a similar modification of an over-simplified understanding of the infallibility of Church teaching.

While the public admission of historical relativity in doctrinal formulations is a recent phenomenon in official Catholicism, one can easily trace modifications of individual doctrines in the Catholic theological handbooks of the last centuries. A particular doctrine that was classified as "a matter of faith" or "proximate to faith" in the manuals of one period may be downgraded to "theologically certain" or "common opinion" in the manuals of a later period. Such a change is often under the impact of new evidence that has caused theologians to re-examine old suppositions. A clear example is the variation in the last 125 years in the presentation of the Church's teaching about evolution. The Church has infallibly taught the doctrine that God was specially involved in creating man in His image and likeness. For almost 1900 years that theological doctrine was interpreted to include the how of man's creation, namely, by direct divine action forming man's body from the earth, and woman's body from man's. Today no serious theologian accepts this understanding of the how, because of the scientific evidence favoring evolution; yet the changed understanding of the how has not negated the infallibility of the Church's teaching, for we have learned to distinguish between the theological insight and the physical imagery in which it was clothed.[7]

---

[6] See p. 19 below.

[7] A common explanation is that the infallible teaching against evolution involved only a rejection of the evolution of man's soul, not of his body. However, such a distinction is post-factum—the strong scientific evidence for the evolution of man's body forced Christians to back down in their rejection of evolution and to dis-

Now, how does this recognition of the limitations of past doctrinal formulations, whether the recognition be explicit or tacit, enter into our reflections on the future of Catholic biblical studies in this century and into the discussion of the two topics treated in this book? If the exact import of doctrinal statements is constantly subject to reexamination and precision in the light of new evidence,[8] for our times the results of biblical criticism constitute an important body of new evidence. (To be sure, these modern results are also time-conditioned and have an element of uncertainty, but that is no excuse for pretending that they can be ignored until some mythical future day when absolute certainty is possible. No greater certitude should be demanded of the biblical criticism of today than was demanded of the biblical criticism of those past times in which the doctrines in question were formulated.) Because of the prominence of this new biblical knowledge it is inevitable that the Church doctrines most likely to be rethought are the doctrines in which biblical data have played a role. It is no accident, then, that under reexamination today are the doctrines

---

tinguish between the evolution of the body and the evolution of the soul.

[8] Occasionally one meets the objection that one cannot admit such reexaminations because they imply that the Church is certain of nothing and that Christians cannot be bound to any profession of faith if our understandings of doctrine might change. This type of theological "domino theory" whereby to reexamine one doctrine threatens all belief is convincing only in a logical vacuum sealed off from history. It is a *fact* of history that we have reexamined and reunderstood doctrines. This did not destroy the Christian faith precisely because, whether explicitly or implicitly, such changes of understanding made it clear that Christian revelation, like its Master, is incarnate—it is the word of God in the words of men; and man's expression of truth is always limited. A Christian is bound to neither more nor less than the acceptance of God's revelation as it is understood and taught in his time. He may know that a particular revelation as he accepts it was not so understood in the past; he may suspect that a particular revelation as he accepts it will not be so understood in the future; but in faith he must leave such variations to God's providence which deals with men of different times in different ways.

of creation, of original sin, of the incarnation and human nature of Jesus, and of the origins of Church ministry and sacraments —all of which are affected by the modern approach to the Bible. My own recent writings have been in this vein. In *Jesus God and Man* I discussed the light that our present scriptural stance throws upon the Church's gradual proclamation of the divinity of Jesus and upon the problems of his knowledge as man. In *Priest and Bishop* I pointed out the challenge raised by NT studies to a simplified understanding of the origins of the priesthood at the Last Supper and the origins of the episcopate through a chain of ordination from the Twelve apostles. As I have mentioned the present volume is prompted by questioners who are wondering whether the biblical evidence, as it is seen today, should cause us to rethink two other doctrines that are deeply biblical in their background: the virginal conception of Jesus and his bodily resurrection.

In my discussion I shall simply present in each case the evidence as I see it. I do not pretend that all Catholic or all Christian critical exegetes will look at it in the same way, but I do hope that the way in which I look at the evidence is scientifically respectable.[9] The evidence must be considered seriously in the Church's ultimate decision on whether our ancient understanding of these two great christological events, the conception and resurrection of Jesus, remains valid and adequate for our times or needs to be modified. To some any thought of modification in our understanding of an ancient doctrine is equivalent to abandoning the doctrine. Yet, as indicated above, Catholic theologians now accept a change in the ancient doctrine of how God created man in order to allow for His having

---

[9] I welcome criticism of this book or of my other books that help me to see the inevitable defects that occur in any scholar's studies. The fundamentalist tendency, however, to question a scholar's faith or his intentions is scarcely a scholarly discussion. In such attacks what is really involved is not a challenge to his scholarship but a challenge to his presuppositions—namely, in my case, that the Scriptures must be approached critically and not simply as history, and that Catholic doctrines are open to restudy and possibly to reformulation. As indicated above, these presuppositions are clearly affirmed by recent popes, Pius XII and John XXIII respectively.

created through a process of evolution—the change in the how has not destroyed the doctrine of creation. Can we be sure *from the start* that there cannot be a similar change in the understanding of the two doctrines under consideration here? We believe that God intervened in the conception of His Son—are we thereby perpetually committed to the notion held in times past of the biological how of that conception, namely, a *virginal* conception? We believe that after His Son's death God intervened by exalting Jesus to His right hand and giving him the name which is above every other name (Philip 2:9)—are we thereby perpetually committed to the notion held in times past of the biological how of that exaltation, namely, a *bodily* resurrection? Although some Catholics are beginning to answer no to these questions (often, I suspect, on the basis of a distrust of the miraculous), it will become apparent that I am not at all inclined in that direction. But neither am I inclined to *a priori* yes on the basis of uncritical affirmations that formulations of Catholic doctrine cannot change. A responsible answer to these questions must take into account the evidence as scholars view it today.

Notice that what I ask is that the answer *take into account* the scholarly evidence. It would be sheer nonsense for me to pretend that scholars can give the Catholic answer to these questions. When it is a question of doctrinal teaching, it is the Church through its various organs of teaching and belief that gives the answer. Thus I offer here no ammunition for the charge that theological scholars are usurping the rights of the magisterium of the Church by their investigations of past doctrines with an eye to possible modification. For the most part theologians are quite aware that the evidence they offer must be assessed within the wider context of the Church's life guided by the Spirit and are only too happy to put their evidence at the service of the magisterium. Indeed it seems to me that in modifying doctrine the magisterium has tacitly recognized the importance of the opinions of theologians; for it tends to make its decisions not by new affirmations but simply by widespread tolerance of corrective views. Thus, in the instance I cited, it would be foolish for us to expect that the Church authorities will pronounce that man's body has evolved from a lower animal form; but the fact that Catholic theologians are allowed to teach this widely indicates *de facto* a change in the Catholic position.[10]

If there is any danger today to the teaching prerogatives of the magisterium, curiously enough it comes less from liberal theologians and more from the Catholic right which loudly condemns discussions of doctrine that open up the possibility of modification or change. The ultimate doctrinal power of the magisterium is to declare a teaching heretical or intolerable within the bounds of Catholic faith. Precisely because of its understanding of the nuanced situation brought about by historical criticism, the teaching authority of the Church has been most reluctant in the last years to categorize modern biblical and theological investigations as heretical. But no such modesty of judgment is attested in the ever-increasing number of right-wing Catholic magazines and newspapers. With the conviction that they are protecting the faith, fundamentalist editorial and column writers hurl charges of heresy and Modernism at attempts, no matter how careful, to apply contemporary biblical or historical criticism to Catholic doctrines. When the official teachers of the Church fail to go along with such condemnations, a ready explanation is offered: the bishops and the Pope are so busy with Church government that they do not keep abreast of the perfidious heresies abroad.

If right-wing vigilanteeism represents a real usurpation of Church authority, it also represents a danger for the continuing progress of Catholic biblical studies in this century, especially since, as I have explained, a main thrust of these studies

---

[10] Of course, this method of procedure gives literalists an advantage, since it means that we rarely have a public Church admission that a change has taken place. Ultra-rightists can keep quoting past statements long after these statements are no longer representative of where the Church actually stands. I wonder how long it was after the Galileo crisis before all Catholics could admit to themselves that, despite the condemnation of Galileo, they were really free to hold that the earth moved around the sun. Books propounding this theory were still refused an imprimatur over two hundred years after the condemnation!

will be to help in the clarification of Catholic doctrine for our times. But for us to turn back in fear at the moment when biblical criticism has graduated from an assimilation of facts to an active influence on the life and thought of the Church would be to frustrate the vision of Pius XII who may well prove to be the greatest Pope-theologian of the century.

And there is clear evidence that the highest Church authority is not at all inclined to abandon Pius' vision by acceding to the obscurantist demands for the suppression of critical biblical and theological discussion. A lesson may be learned from the enlightened way that Rome has recently dealt with one of the problems treated in this book, the problem of the bodily resurrection. Knowing that there were new views abroad, some of them disturbing, the Roman authorities made no attempt to condemn scholarly opinions or to forbid discussion. Rather they saw that by lending patronage to an honest scholarly discussion, they could encourage the scholars themselves to promote sound views and criticize unsound ones. And so a group of Catholic scholars who had written some of the most trenchant studies on the resurrection were invited at Easter time, 1970, to meet in Rome and to present papers that would ultimately be published by the Vatican Press. I was brought over from the United States for this meeting, and some of the reflections in Chapter Two below stem from the perceptive studies and remarks I heard on the occasion. Fundamentalists opposed to modern Catholic biblical studies would have been scandalized, were they present, to observe the virtual unanimity with which the scholars accepted a critical modification of the historicity of the post-resurrectional Gospel accounts. But it was precisely to see where Catholic scholars were in agreement that the meeting was called. At its close Pope Paul VI received the scholars in private audience and spoke these words: [11]

---

[11] *L'Osservatore Romano* of April 5, 1970. Translated from the French.

We thank the Lord for this meeting that He has granted us with highly qualified specialists in exegesis, theology, and philosophy, who have come to share fraternally their investigations into the mystery of the resurrection of Christ. ... We observe with great respect the hermeneutical and exegetical work that qualified men of science, such as you, accomplish in relation to this fundamental theme.... The Church itself encounters the difficulties inherent in the exegesis of unclear and difficult texts and knows the usefulness of having diverse opinions.... Therefore be full of confidence in the security of the tradition that the Church guarantees with her magisterium—the Church who continues to encourage scientific study, at the same time that she continues to proclaim the faith of the apostles.

(B) Basic Biblical Suppositions

If the current of biblical studies, as well as the invitation of Church authorities, impels scholars to discuss such sensitive doctrinal subjects as the virginal conception and the bodily resurrection, I recognize with concern that some of the readers attracted by such a discussion may be ill-equipped to understand the methods of modern biblical criticism. I could warn such readers that the problems discussed in this book are best studied only after one is familiar with current approaches to the main Gospel story stretching from Jesus' baptism to his death. Nevertheless, I think it wiser to face the possibility that such a warning will not dissuade, and so I shall spell out some biblical assumptions that are basic to my treatment.

(1) The OT authors did not foresee in detail the life of Jesus of Nazareth. Those who are called OT prophets were concerned with their own times and not with the distant future about which they could speak only in the vaguest way. Therefore, whether they know it or not, when the NT authors see prophecy fulfilled in Jesus, they are going beyond the vision of the OT authors.[12] Let us take, for instance, Isa 7:14: "A

---

[12] The classic apologetic argument from prophecy has had to be reinterpreted in the light of modern biblical criticism. It is no longer

young woman shall be [or is] with child and shall bear a son and shall call him Immanuel." The prophet was referring to the birth of a child taking place some seven hundred years before Jesus' time, a child whose coming into the world was a sign of the continuance of the royal Davidic line. Because Matthew regarded Jesus as the completion of this royal Davidic line, and because he read the passage in a Greek translation of Isaiah which spoke of a "virgin" (as distinct from the Hebrew which has only "young woman"), Matthew saw the applicability of this text to the birth of Jesus from the Virgin Mary at Bethlehem. It was a proof for Matthew who had an insight as to how Jesus' birth fulfilled God's plan; but, so far as we can tell, Isaiah knew nothing or foresaw nothing about Jesus' birth. Similarly, Hosea 6:2, "After two days he will revive us; on the third day he will raise us up," in the prophet's mind had nothing to do with the resurrection of Jesus. The likeness to the NT theme of the resurrection of Jesus on the third day (I Cor 15:4) *may* have arisen because the NT authors deliberately phrased their remembrance of the resurrection in the language of Hosea.[13]

(2) The Gospel accounts of the ministry of Jesus were written anywhere from thirty to sixty years after the events they narrate. The evangelists were second-generation Christians who had not been eyewitnesses themselves. I accept the common scholarly opinion that Mark was the first of our written Gospels (composed in the 60's?). The author of the Gospel that we call "according to Matthew" was not Matthew the tax collector and companion of Jesus, but an unknown Christian who used as his source Mark's Gospel (and other traditions) and who may have written in the 80's. Luke's Gospel may be dated to the 80's, give or take ten years, and is also dependent in part on Mark. John's Gospel was not written by the son of Zebedee nor by the Beloved Disciple (if he was not the son of Zebedee),

primarily a question of the exact fulfillment of divinely guided foreknowledge; it is much more a question of the culmination of a divine plan that could only be detected through hindsight.

[13] See n. 210 below.

but by an unknown Christian who was a follower or disciple of the Beloved Disciple. In its final form it was probably written in the 90's. Although not eyewitnesses themselves, the evangelists drew upon early traditions about Jesus.

(3) In the process of development from Jesus through the early traditions to the evangelists,[14] there was considerable growth in the Gospel message and content. The Gospels, then, are not simply factual reporting of what happened in Jesus' ministry but are documents of faith written to show the significance of those events as seen with hindsight. As an example of what that might mean for our purposes in this book, the fact that according to the Synoptic (first three) Gospels Jesus predicted his crucifixion and resurrection three times and in increasing detail (Mark 8:31; 9:31; 10:33-34) does not necessarily mean that the historical Jesus had such exact foreknowledge of his future. Actually Jesus may have made more general statements expressing an assurance that God would not desert him but would make him victorious;[15] and, knowing the outcome of his

---

[14] This process of Gospel development is spelled out for Catholics in *Dei Verbum* (v 19) of Vatican II and in more detail in the 1964 Pontifical Biblical Commission Instruction "On the Historical Truth of the Gospels" (conveniently available in a Paulist Press pamphlet with an important commentary by J. A. Fitzmyer). The instruction distinguished three stages: the work of the historical Jesus, the period of the apostolic preachers, and the period of the sacred writers. It pointed out that there was already a tremendous development in the apostolic period because after the resurrection a perception of Jesus' divinity colored the memory of what he had said and done. And the sacred writers not only selected and synthesized the traditions that came down from the apostles—they also "explicated" those traditions in light of the church situations. Thus it would be within the lines laid down by official Church teaching to interpret words attributed to Jesus in the Gospels as examples of explication by the evangelists, if our evidence warranted such a conclusion.

[15] For instance we may compare to the detailed predictions in Mark the three vague predictions in John about the "lifting up" of the Son of Man (3:14, 8:28, 12:32-34). For the reasons why scholars think that the details of the Marcan predictions were supplied by the Church rather than coming from Jesus, see J. Jeremias,

life, Church preachers and the evangelists may have reformulated those statements and supplied detail in light of the actual occurrences of the passion. An obvious objection is that, even if the evangelists themselves were not eyewitnesses, the continued survival of eyewitnesses would have prevented much creative development in the Gospel tradition over such a short period of thirty to sixty years. This argument cannot be discounted as support for the general lines of Gospel historicity, but it will not hold for many details in the Gospel accounts. In our times, despite the much greater control exercised by exact written and oral records, we have seen a tremendous growth in the tradition about figures such as Pope John and John F. Kennedy within ten years after their death, so that one can speak of a difference between these men as they were in history and as they are in the popular evaluation.

(4) The belief that the Sacred Scriptures are inspired by God does not mean that they are necessarily factually exact. Inspiration means that God guided the composition of the biblical books.[16] This is an affirmation of faith, and it cannot be tested by empirical criteria. What can be tested for scientific

New Testament Theology (New York: Scribners, 1971), pp. 277-86; and G. Strecker, "The Passion and Resurrection Predictions in Mark's Gospel," _Interpretation_ 22 (1968) 421-42.

[16] Past definitions and descriptions of inspiration in Catholic circles were often very simple in their presuppositions about how the biblical books were composed, as if most biblical books had only one author upon whose mind God worked. In fact, many of the biblical books represent tradition collected over centuries, involving many men in different degrees of authorship and indeed, at times, involving a whole community. For this reason, recent Catholic scholars have been shying away from attempts at exact definitions of inspiration until there is time to digest all that we have learned about the Scriptures. The study of inspiration must be much more _a posteriori_ than it was previously. On the basis of a theory about how God acted we should not determine what happened in Scripture; we should rather study what actually appears in the Scriptures and work back from that to a theory of God's action that would explain what happened.

exactitude is the end product, the Scriptures. From our study of
the Bible we can see that it consists of different types of literature, akin to the literatures of other ancient peoples. (The
Bible's uniqueness is in its theological profundity and not simply
in literary style.) Within the Bible are historical writings of
varying degrees of accuracy, poems epic and lyrical, sermons,
letters, parables, fiction, etc. As the Constitution on Divine
Revelation of Vatican II insisted (*Dei Verbum,* iii 12), anyone who wishes to discover the intention of the biblical writer
must pay attention to such "literary forms." Each style of literature must be judged for accuracy according to its own standards;
and so, sweeping statements about the inerrancy of the Bible
are inapplicable. Biblical fiction and parable (books like Judith,
Esther, Jonah) remain fiction and parable even though the
composition was inspired by God; inspiration does not turn
fiction and parable into history. As we have said, the Second
Vatican Council reversed a tendency of applying inerrancy
to almost every aspect of the Bible and applied it only in a very
general way: "The books of Scripture must be acknowledged
as teaching firmly, faithfully, and *without error* that truth which
God wanted put into the sacred writings for the sake of our
salvation" (*Dei Verbum,* iii 11).

The recognition that the Bible can be fallible as regards
details of historical accuracy is very important for the logic of
our discussions in this book. For instance, we shall see that the
various Gospels give different reports of what happened at the
empty tomb of Jesus, especially in the details of the angelic
appearances. In the past Catholic scholars have spent much
energy trying to harmonize these diverse accounts, often with
the supposition that they must preserve the historical accuracy
of each. Today we would be free to say that one or all the
accounts have been influenced and shaped by popular imagination during the stage of oral transmission and also by the
editorial goals of the sacred writer who used earlier traditions.
Again, Matthew and Luke give very different accounts of Jesus'
conception and birth. In times past we would have assumed that,
because these infancy stories were recounted by inspired writers,
both were accurate and had to be harmonized. Today, *if the*

evidence is strong enough, we would be free to consider either or both of the narratives as not historical. Obviously this is a conclusion that should not be reached quickly; but we cannot deny *a priori* the possibility that, since there were no apostolic eyewitnesses for the events accompanying the birth of Jesus,[17] traditions about that birth *could* have been produced by popular imagination. As for the inerrancy of the empty tomb narratives and the infancy narratives (even if the stories themselves prove to be imaginative in whole or in part), we must work with the criterion supplied by Vatican II: from the overall import of these narratives what did God want taught through them for the sake of our salvation? That would be inerrant.

With the above groundrules let us proceed to our discussion of two of the most debated Gospel problems of our times.

---

[17] In this aspect the infancy narratives are different from the majority of the material reported in the Gospels for which there could have been apostolic eyewitnesses. Obviously the infancy narratives *could* rest on family witness, e.g., that of Mary or of Joseph; but, as we shall see, there is no persuasive evidence for such witness. As for the objection that even without eyewitness testimony the evangelists were closer to the birth events than we are and therefore would have known whether or not they were dealing with reliable traditions, I submit that this is not always true when we think in terms of historical method. The nuance in the question "What exactly happened?" is just as modern as queries we might make about the exact medical diagnosis of diseases mentioned in the Gospels. Luke, purportedly a physician, was much closer to information about the diseases Jesus encountered in his ministry than is any doctor today; but on the basis of the material reported, even at a distance of nearly two thousand years, a modern doctor could give a better medical diagnosis than could Luke. There is often a similar competency for the modern exegete with his critical methods in the type of scientific historical investigation on which we are embarked.

CHAPTER ONE
THE PROBLEM OF THE
VIRGINAL CONCEPTION
OF JESUS[18]

In a certain sense this is not one of the most relevant problems of theology or exegesis. The solution to it will not help the wretched in the inner city or even the wretched in the suburbs; should it be resolved, there will remain questions of war and peace and even of priestly celibacy. To some the problem will seem a parade example of the purely (or impurely) inquisitive in theology, in short, the "nosey."[19] Yet, in another sense,

---

[18] In its original form, subsequently published in *Theological Studies* 33 (1972), 3-34 (to which grateful acknowledgment is given), this chapter was delivered in the James Memorial Chapel of Union Theological Seminary (N. Y. C.) on Nov. 18, 1971 as an inaugural lecture on the occasion of the author's becoming Auburn Professor of Biblical Studies, a joint appointment of Union Seminary and Woodstock College. The occasion of republication has permitted the expansion of some sections. The author initiated his reflection on this topic in giving the Swander Lectures at Lancaster Theological Seminary (April 1971) and the Boylan Lecture at University College, Dublin (July 1971), for which opportunities of refining and maturing his thought he expresses his gratitude. He also notes a debt to Walter J. Burghardt, S. J., for having made available the documentation pertinent to the Dutch controversy about the virginal conception. The ecumenical perspective appropriate to the original setting of the lecture has been preserved here.

[19] Some would equate the theologically relevant with what is

is it ever irrelevant to be nosey about Jesus, especially when our inquisitiveness touches on his uniqueness? Unless there is something unique about the way "God was in Christ reconciling the world to Himself" (II Cor 5:19), even the most "relevant" Christian theology becomes irrelevant.

I. The State of the Problem

In Protestantism the question of the virginal conception has been debated for a long time. In some quarters it has been settled with a negative response about historicity, a response occasionally accompanied with a perceptive hesitancy that the negation threatens a symbolism touching on the mystery of Christ. In other quarters an affirmative answer remains one of the essential criteria of orthodoxy, so that English Bibles which do not carry the word "virgin" in Isa 7:14 are suspect. In still other quarters the subject is discreetly avoided, except perhaps by a nervous examination board testing a candidate's doctrinal suitability for the ministry. Since the denial of the virginal conception was initiated by the rationalists, there remains a certain suspicion about those who hesitate to evaluate it as a historical fact. And so it may well be that a reconsideration of the evidence will be of utility in the broad span of Protestantism.

In Roman Catholicism (and Eastern Orthodoxy) there has been a unanimity in regarding the historicity of the virginal conception as unquestionable. But after Vatican II the solid front is cracking in many places. As with so many other issues the questioning has been more public in the Netherlands than

---

essential for being identified as a Christian; and our question fares poorly if one asks: Do you mean that a man who believes in Jesus is not able to be called a Christian because he does not think that Jesus was born of a virgin? No matter how one may answer that question (and most would not be inclined to answer it with a "yes"), it is disastrous to reduce Christian theology or belief to the minimum. A more pertinent question is: Is a thinking Christian loyal to his heritage when he denies that Jesus was born of a virgin?

elsewhere.[20] In 1965-66 J. van Kilsdonk, a Jesuit who served as chaplain for the students at the University of Amsterdam, attracted attention when he voiced his opinion that a biological understanding of the virginal conception is a barrier to genuine christology, is prejudicial to belief in the incarnation, and does not correspond to the scriptural affirmation.[21] Almost at the same time the famous "Dutch Catechism" raised eyebrows by its ambiguity on the factuality of the virginal conception.[22] It told Catholic believers that by proclaiming that "Jesus' birth was not due to the will of a man," Matthew and Luke were expressing the theological truth that Jesus was born wholly of grace and was *the* gift of God. "They proclaim that this birth does not depend on what men can do of themselves—infinitely less so than in other human births. That is the deepest meaning of the article of faith, 'born of the Virgin Mary.' " No one could fault what the Catechism said, but many noticed what it did *not* say explicitly, namely, that Jesus was born of a woman who was biologically a virgin. And so, despite the imprimatur of Cardinal Alfrink, the orthodoxy of the Catechism came under attack. The Dutch bishops who had composed a foreword for it subsequently made an effort, as it were, to make one thing perfectly clear: they did not intend any ambiguity about Mary's corporeal virginity.[23] They cited as a truth "which the Church

---

[20] Almost simultaneously there was difficulty in Germany over the case of Peter Lengsfeld, a priest Dozent at Münster, who taught that in the light of the biblical evidence it could no longer be denied with certainty that Joseph was the physical father of Jesus. The displeasure this aroused in the German Catholic hierarchy delayed Lengsfeld's promotion to a professorship.

[21] Initially, Van Kilsdonk expressed himself in a student newspaper of Dec. 3, 1965; this led to an interrogation in Rome on July 4, 1966. Not deterred by this nor by the statement of the Dutch Bishops (note 23 below), Van Kilsdonk reiterated his views in a radio interview on Oct. 11, 1966.

[22] See pp. 74-75 of the English edition: *A New Catechism, Catholic Faith for Adults* (New York: Herder and Herder, 1967).

[23] A statement from the bishops' meeting in Utrecht was published in the Amsterdam newspaper *De Tijd* (Aug. 19, 1966).

has always believed and proclaimed on the basis of the Gospel"
the virginal conception of Jesus in the sense that he "was born
of the Virgin Mary through the overshadowing of the Holy
Spirit, without a man's cooperation." Rome showed enough
concern about the Catechism to appoint a commission of cardinals to investigate complaints. The result[24] was a corrected text
of the Catechism which insists that Jesus "was not procreated
by the intervention of man."

This did not stop the controversy which has now spread to
other countries. Rosemary Ruether caused considerable dis-
turbance in her column in the American Catholic press when
she questioned the virginity of Mary, arguing that in the infancy
narratives the theme of virginal conception was a secondary
development in relation to an earlier and probably more historical tradition of Joseph's physical paternity.[25] As other examples
of how this trend is making headway among Catholics I would
cite the latest scholarly treatment of the question in Germany
which seems to classify the virginal conception of Jesus as a
theologoumenon,[26] and the facile remarks of Louis Evely who

---

[24] *Acta Apostolicae Sedis* 60 (1968), 688, reports a directive that
the Catechism "must teach equally clearly [with the perpetual virginity of Mary] the doctrine of the virginal birth of Jesus, which is
so supremely in accord with the mystery of the incarnation. No
further occasion shall be given for denying this truth . . . retaining
only a symbolic meaning [of virginal birth], for instance, that it
merely expresses the gift inspired by pure grace that God bestowed
upon us in His Son." The resulting corrected text of the Catechism
is now printed as a supplement.

[25] Her argument is stated in fuller form in "The Collision of His-
tory and Doctrine: The Brothers of Jesus and the Virginity of
Mary," *Continuum* 7 (1969), 93-105. Much of the article concerns
Mary's continuing virginity after Jesus' birth, and that problem is
the focus of the response by A. J. Novak, "The Virgin Birth: *Ad
Ruether*," *Continuum* 7 (1969), 443-52.

[26] In the collection *Zum Thema Jungfrauengeburt* (Stuttgart:
Katholisches Bibelwerk, 1970) by K. S. Frank, R. Kilian, *et al.,*
the article on Matthew's infancy narrative by O. Knoch, p. 58,
raises this possibility. For him a "theologoumenon" would mean
that the belief that Jesus was God's Son in a unique sense has been
historicized (made *geschichtlich*) in the infancy narratives where

dismisses it as a "maladroit fable."[27] In a British catechetical magazine published with ecclesiastical approval it is stated: "Many of them [Catholics] imagine that to doubt the fact that Jesus was conceived and born of a virgin is to undermine a fundamental truth of faith. . . . The virgin birth would seem to remain an open question; it is in any case, as said above, of secondary importance."[28] The December 1972 issue of the

---

he has no human father. Evidently Knoch agrees with J. Michl, "Die Jungfrauengeburt im Neuen Testament," *Mariologische Studien* 4 (1969), 145-84, who maintains (p. 183) that historico-critical exegesis cannot resolve the problem of whether the virginal conception of Jesus is a historical fact or a theologoumenon. In the article on Luke's infancy narrative, G. Lattke, p. 88, treats the virginal conception as the development of theological reflection rather than the reminiscence of a historical happening.

We should note that authors who use the term "theologoumenon" in relation to the virginal conception are not necessarily agreed about the degree of non-historicity to be attributed to the picture in which the theological truth finds expression. It seems to me that three questions would have to be asked of those who claim that the virginal conception is the historicizing of the truth that Jesus is God's Son. (a) Is it this truth that the virginal conception actually conveys in the NT, especially in Matthew which seems to put primary emphasis on answering calumny, on affirming Davidic descent, and on fulfillment of prophecy? (b) Do we have reason to think that it would occur to early Christians to express divine sonship in terms of virginal conception? Is this an imagery that would suggest itself to Jewish believers in Jesus, whether Greek-speaking or Semitic-speaking? (c) Even if the answers to both *a* and *b* are affirmative, does this prove that, in fact, a virginal conception did not occur?

[27] L. Evely, *The Gospels Without Myth* (Garden City: Doubleday, 1971), pp. 80-82. "The belief in Mary's physical virginity is based on the need to translate the mystery of the Incarnation into terms intelligible to unsophisticated people."

[28] F. Somerville, "Life and Ministry of Jesus," *The Sower* 264 (July 1972), 84. It is probably inaccurate to describe the problem of the virginal conception as an open question for Catholics. Although I claim no expertise in catechetics, I would maintain that the question is not an "open" one *on the catechetical level,* for the theological discussion is too inchoate to have had any effect on the Church's official teaching which is at the core of religious instruc-

Ladies' Home Journal discusses theological views on Mary, and on p. 127 a Catholic professor states that, while the Church officially regards the virginal conception literally, "most theologians today look at it symbolically." Even if we allow for the sensationalism of a popular magazine, we must face the fact of increasingly propagandized doubt.

Thus, there is a growing need for a careful discussion of the problem by Catholic theologians, historians, and exegetes, hopefully in cooperation with their Protestant confreres. Some Catholics will resent such a discussion, charging that the participants are denying the virginal conception; but then no one has yet discovered a protection against the calumny of oversimplification. Indubitably, the accusation of pastoral irresponsibility will be leveled on the grounds that any discussion of the virginal conception, no matter how carefully conducted, will disturb the faithful. The above history of Catholic denials of the virginal conception, however, indicates a trend that is bound to have disturbing effects on the faithful. For competent Catholic scholars to avoid the discussion is not prudence but cowardice;[29]

---

tion. At most, those involved in religious instruction might indicate to their pupils that theologians are grappling with new factors in this area, as indeed in most other areas. Nor does it seem to me that the problem of the virginal conception is an open question *in Catholic theology* if "open" is understood to mean that a sizeable number of theologians think that an affirmative or a negative answer is equally possible. As I shall indicate, in the past Catholic theologians have classified an affirmative answer as the infallible teaching of the Church. What is true is that some are asking how accurate such a classification was and whether further discussion is foreclosed. Perhaps this is all that Somerville means by "open question."

[29] In the time since I did the research for my lecture in 1971, scholarly Catholic attention to the problem of the virginal conception is increasing, e.g., P. Schoonenberg and J. M. Alonso, "La concepción virginal de Jesús, historia o leyenda? Un diálogo teológico," *Ephemerides Mariologicae* 21 (1971), 161-216; J. M. Alonso, "Boletin de Mariologia: Cuestiones actuales II: La concepción virginal entre católicos," *Ibid.*, pp. 257-302; P. Grelot, "La

for they will turn the field over to irresponsible popularizers like Evely, who resurrects the rationalistic positions of the last century, thinking he is biblically *au courant.*

Before proceeding further, it would be wise for me to specify carefully the question under consideration. I am concerned with the belief that Jesus was conceived in the womb of a virgin without the intervention of a human father, i.e., without male seed; and every time I use the expression "virginal conception," I use it in that sense.[30] I have chosen "virginal conception" rather than "virgin birth" in order not to confuse this matter with another, somewhat recondite belief concerning the miraculous *birth* of Jesus or the way he emerged from the womb.[31] Nor do I enter here into the question of still another aspect of Mary's virginity, namely, her lifetime virginity or the view held

---

naissance d'Isaac et celle de Jésus," *Nouvelle Revue Théologique* 94 (1972), 462-87, 561-85; A. Vögtle, "Offene Fragen zur lukanischen Geburts- und Kindheitsgeschichte," *Bibel und Leben* 11 (1970), 51-67 (an article I had previously overlooked). The topic, then, is being discussed by Catholic scholars in Spanish, French, and German—it is a sad commentary that the prospect of such a discussion by an American Catholic scholar caused outrage and hysteria among Catholic fundamentalists in this country.

[30] It is a question, then, of the "bodily" or "biological" virginity of Mary in conceiving Jesus (the former term having the advantage of being less clinical). Of course, even if this aspect is in direct focus, the question still has a converse side: Was the conception of Jesus by a unique action of God, an action differing from His general providence in the conception of other men? If later God uniquely freed Jesus from the bonds of death, a privilege not yet accorded to other men, was such an eschatological power effective already in the conception of Jesus?

[31] In classical mariology a threefold virginity has been attributed to Mary: *ante partum, in partu, et post partum.* (Triadic patterns can be traced back to about A.D. 370 and Zeno of Verona: *Tractatus* I, 5, 3 and II, 8, 2; *PL* 11, 303, and 414-15.) By virginal conception I mean *virginitas ante partum.* Usually the miracle of *virginitas in partu* has been specified in terms of birth without rupture of the hymen and/or birth without pain. See Karl Rahner, *Theological Reflections* IV (Baltimore: Helicon, 1966), 134-62.

by many Christians that she had neither marital relations nor children after the birth of Jesus.[32] (Obviously, however, a negative answer given to the question of the virginal conception of Jesus would render meaningless any discussion of Mary's subsequent virginity, whether in giving miraculous birth or in refraining from marital relations.) In confining myself to the virginal conception I am treating the only aspect of Mary's virginity that is directly scriptural.

I am aware, however, that in raising the question of Mary's *bodily* virginity I am not corresponding to the primary emphasis of the evangelists. Matthew and Luke are interested in virginal conception as a sign of divine choice and grace, and as the idiom of a christological insight that Jesus was God's Son or the Davidic Messiah from birth, etc.—in other words, they are interested in it as a phenomenon with theological import.[33] Nevertheless, when one recognizes the primacy of the theological implications (perhaps by using terminology like "theological" or "spiritual" virginity), the question of historicity is still a legitimate one. Some theologians can continue to speak of "virgin birth," even though they think that the conception of Jesus was through marital intercourse. For other theologians that term refers to a conception that really was virginal and not natural. Still others use the term "virgin birth" but consider the question of bodily virginity of no import, and they are willing to take an agnostic stance toward it.[34] The purpose of my

---

[32] The doctrine of *virginitas post partum* depends on how one understands the family relationship implied in the references to Jesus' brothers (and sisters) in Mark 6:3; Matt 13:55; and John 2:12, 7:5. Were they siblings (Tertullian, Helvidius, modern Protestants); or were they stepbrothers (Epiphanius) or cousins (Hegesippus, Jerome, principal Reformers)? See J. Blinzler, *Die Brüder und Schwestern Jesu* (Stuttgart: Katholisches Bibelwerk, 1967).

[33] See P. Minear, "The Interpreter and the Birth Narratives," *Symbolae Biblicae Upsalienses* 13 (1950), 1-22.

[34] As an example of flexibility let me cite Floyd W. Filson, *A New Testament History* (Philadelphia: Westminster, 1964), p. 86: "Here God was at work to bring into human life the one who was to carry out God's unique saving purpose for men. Whatever may be thought of the physical origin of Jesus, whether he had a human

inquiry is to determine which is the most responsible of these various attitudes, all of which rightly accent the theological import but disagree on the underlying historical fact (the manner of the conception).

Inevitably, no matter how hard one may try to be objective in such an inquiry, there are certain predispositions toward a particular solution. In times past the predispositions would have been favorable toward the historicity of the virginal conception. It was expected that the marvelous should accompany God's actions among men, and the miraculous supported faith. In recent times, however, the miraculous has created suspicion among many Christians. This is more than mere rationalism or the association of the miraculous with the credulous. Rather it stems from an appreciation of what is truly unique in the Judeo-Christian religion, namely, a conviction that God has been operative in human history, a history like our own. A history studded with the miraculous is not the history we live in. And so recent predispositions have run against the thesis that Jesus, who was like us in all but sin, should have been conceived differently from other men.[35]

Yet we cannot let predispositions govern the discussion. And, indeed, there are signs of a changing attitude toward the

---

father or not, his coming and career cannot be explained by reference to human parentage and heritage.... If he had a human father, that does not exclude the unique action of God to bring this life into the world."

[35] Even in antiquity there was an instinctive reluctance to make the virginal conception appear too marvelous, too unique. Already in Origen, *Contra Celsum* 1, 37 (*GCS* 2, 88-89), there is a search for analogies in the instances of animal parthenogenesis. And today there are the latest developments in experimental embryology, e.g., cloning, which open the possibility of reproduction without sexual intercourse. Others appeal to the analogy of evolution wherein the first man or men would not have had human parents. However, the quest for natural parallels runs contrary to what the evangelists are emphasizing; for they stress the role of the Holy Spirit and regard the virginal conception as an act of divine power. For them it is important that God was acting *out of the ordinary way* in bringing about the birth of His Son.

miraculous in biblical research. As an illustration we may reflect upon Rudolf Bultmann's treatment of the Gospel miracles; for him they were for the most part a later and non-historical addendum to the Jesus-tradition supplied by Christian miracle-story tellers who were trying to make the picture of Jesus competitive in a world that expected the miraculous. Naturally, he had exegetical arguments for his position, but the decisive factor in his outlook was his contention that modern man does not believe in miracles. But today Ernst Käsemann, one of Bultmann's most renowned pupils, has shifted from the stance of his master. He maintains that, since exorcisms (those miracles that seem so totally foreign to modern man) are found in the earliest strata of our information about Jesus, then if one wishes to remain a historian, one must accept the historicity of the tradition that Jesus was an exorcist.[36] And so, analogously, if we are to enter this discussion as historians and theologians and exegetes, it cannot be an answer for us that modern man does not believe in virginal conceptions, any more than it can be an answer that, since Christians of the past accepted the virginal conception, we must follow in their footsteps blindly. Both the rationalist and the traditionalist must be open to an honest attempt to survey the evidence—and it may well be that the former will find this more threatening than the latter. Let us turn, then, to the evidence, which we shall discuss under four headings: the evidence from authority; the evidence from interlocking doctrines; the evidence from early history; the evidence from the Scriptures.

---

[36] Quoted in Norman Perrin, *Rediscovering the Teaching of Jesus* (New York: Harper, 1967), p. 65. Perrin himself observes: "Today this would be a widely accepted consensus of critical opinion." Of course, all NT scholarship did not go the route of Bultmannian skepticism about the miracle tradition and subsequent reappreciation —see my article "The Gospel Miracles," *New Testament Essays* (Milwaukee: Bruce, 1965), pp. 168-91, or pp. 218-45 in the Doubleday Image reprint.

II. The Evidence from Authority

For some Christians supreme authority in matters of belief resides in the Bible as the word of God; for other Christians such authority is vested in the teachings of a living Church, teachings of which the Bible is a part. The wide acceptance of the virginal conception stems from its being presented as part of the Christian heritage both in the Bible and in Church pronouncements. Yet this unanimity does not foreclose the question; for modern theological insights make it necessary to qualify the authority both of the Bible and of Church teaching, or at least to qualify the way in which that authority is understood to function.

Later I shall return at length to the biblical evidence. Let me note here only that, while Matthew and Luke apparently accepted the virginal conception as historical,[37] we cannot be certain where they got their information on this point.[38] The older thesis that all the information in Luke's infancy narrative came straight from Mary's side of the family, while Matthew's information came from Joseph's side, is no longer tenable in modern exegesis—even though family origins for some information cannot be *a priori* excluded. Consequently, we must face the possibility that in good faith the evangelists have taken over an earlier belief in virginal conception that does not have

---

[37] Even if their interest in the virginal conception was primarily theological, as I have stressed, the evangelists were not sophisticated beyond their times. It is lucidly clear that Matthew believed in Mary's bodily virginity before the birth of Jesus (1:25). It is harder to *prove* the case for Luke; but 3:23 indicates that Luke did not think that Joseph begot Jesus after the angel's annunciation to Mary.

[38] The infancy narratives cannot be compared to the Gospel accounts of Jesus' public ministry. For the latter, the community relied upon a *basis* of eyewitness testimony by the disciples of Jesus, no matter how much the tradition developed in the course of time. But we do not know if eyewitness or close-to-eyewitness testimony stands behind any of the stories pertinent to Jesus' infancy. How many would have been in a position to know the intimate details of Jesus' conception?

an authentic historical basis. In short, the presence of the virginal conception in the infancy narratives of two Gospels carries no absolute guarantee of historicity.[39]

What guarantee of historicity is offered by Church teaching about the virginal conception? The evidence from Church authority reaches back into very old creedal tradition. An early elaboration of the Old Roman Baptismal Creed confesses "Christ Jesus, His only Son, our Lord" as "born from the Holy Spirit and the Virgin Mary." The creed of Nicaea-Constantinople confesses Jesus Christ "who came down and became incarnate from the Holy Spirit and the Virgin Mary." The Apostles' Creed confesses "Jesus Christ, His only Son, our Lord, who was conceived by the Holy Spirit, born from the Virgin Mary." There can be no doubt that those who formulated these creedal affirmations believed in the bodily virginity of Mary. Yet many scholars are convinced that the real thrust of creedally reciting *birth from the Virgin Mary* involved the reality of Jesus' *birth* and his humanity, not the exact "how" of his *conception*.[40] (Thus, "born of the Virgin Mary" would be de-

---

[39] As mentioned on p. 19 above, the Roman Catholic position now sees inerrancy to apply to "that truth which God wanted put into the sacred writings for the sake of our salvation." The human nature and the divine sonship of Jesus are truths gleaned from the infancy narratives which would meet this qualification for inerrant teaching—is the bodily virginity of Mary such a truth?

[40] The new fourth canon of the Roman Mass has caught the precise thrust of the creedal confession, as I indicate by italics: "He was conceived through the power of the Holy Spirit and born of the Virgin Mary—*a man like us* in all things but sin." It is worth emphasizing that the creeds speak of the virgin *birth* not of the virginal conception. I have indicated (see n. 31 above) that in this book I prefer the term "virginal conception" in order to avoid confusion between *virginitas ante partum* and *virginitas in partu*. But there is a second and more important reason for my preference. By speaking of virginal conception I can be precise about the problem of Mary's bodily virginity in a way that is not possible if I fall back on the creedal formulas pertaining to the virgin birth (which also refer to *ante partum,* not to *in partu*), precisely because the latter are almost exclusively christological. An exception would be the long form of the creed of Epiphanius (*DBS* #44; *ca.* A.D.

scended in spirit from the Pauline formula in Gal 4:4, "God sent forth His Son, *born of a woman,* born under the law"— a formula that gives expression to the radical historicity of Jesus and his mission by stressing the fact that he came from a woman's womb, but without emphasizing the manner in which he was conceived in that womb.) More specifically, even before A. D. 200, in the Old Roman Creed the affirmation of belief in Christ Jesus was expanded by a reference to his birth from the Virgin Mary in order to counteract a docetism and gnosticism that questioned the reality of Jesus' humanity.[41] Toward the end of the fourth century the Nicene creedal affirmation about the incarnation was specified in the Constantinopolitan version in terms of incarnation from the Virgin Mary, an insertion possibly aimed at the Apollinarians who did not admit the completeness of Jesus' humanity.[42] And so if we judge the creedal affirmations from what they were meant to refute, it may be asked whether, in speaking of the virgin birth, they ever defined *precisely as a matter of faith* the virginal conception as I have been using that term, even though they certainly presupposed it. If I may resort to technical Roman Catholic theological terms, it may be asked whether the *bodily* virginity of Mary in conceiving Jesus has ever been infallibly

---

374) which is more specific: "He was not born of male seed, nor was he within a man."

[41] J. N. D. Kelly, *Early Christian Creeds* (2 ed.; London: Longmans, 1960), pp. 144-45. Kelly calls attention to "the insistence of this section of the creed on the reality of Christ's human experiences— His birth, His physical sufferings, His death and burial." Of course, the creeds confess birth not only from the Virgin Mary but also from the Holy Spirit, and indeed put the Holy Spirit first to emphasize the divine element in Jesus' incarnation. But my focus of interest here is the "why" of the mention of the Virgin Mary. Docetists might admit that a pre-existent Christ came into the world *through* (*per*) Mary, but not that he was *of* or *from* (*ex, de*) her —flesh of flesh. Of course, there were more than anti-docetic motives for the insertion into the creed of references to Christ's earthly career, for there was an interest in his life as well.

[42] *Ibid.*, pp. 332-38. The anti-Apollinarian thrust is not certain.

defined by the extraordinary magisterium of the Church functioning through its creeds and ecumenical councils.[43]

But we have not seen the whole picture, for the extent of Church authority cannot be confined to the rare statements of the extraordinary magisterium. There is a wider area of matters of divine revelation, not defined by creed or ecumenical council, but proposed consistently and universally with such force that they have been accepted in faith by Christians as a whole —the *ubique, semper, ab omnibus* of Vincent of Lerins, or what in Roman Catholicism would be called an exercise of the ordinary magisterium of the Church. And even if the "how" of Jesus' conception was not the center of the creedal affirmations, the development of mariology did eventually focus the attention of the Christian believer on the bodily virginity of Mary, the ever-virgin.[44] It would seem to me that for some 1600 years of Christian existence (A.D. 200-1800) the virginal conception of Jesus, in a biological sense, was universally believed by

---

[43] There are official Church statements pertaining to the bodily virginity of Mary, but none of them seems to meet the very strict requirements for a *de fide* exercise of the extraordinary magisterium. For instance, (a) in A.D. 449 the letter of Pope Leo I to Bishop Flavian (*DBS* #291) speaks of Mary's having conceived with her virginity intact (*salva virginitate concepit*) and without carnal pleasure. (b) In A.D. 649 the Lateran Council (*DBS* #503) condemned anyone who would not confess that the holy, immaculate, and ever-virgin Mary conceived of the Holy Spirit without seed (*absque semine; asporōs*) and gave birth without detriment to her virginity. (c) In A.D. 675 the Eleventh Council of Toledo (*DBS* #533) spoke of the intact virginity of Mary who did not have intercourse with a man (*intacta virginitas et virilem coitum nescivit*). (d) In A.D. 1555 a bull issued by Pope Paul IV against the antitrinitarians and Socinians (*DBS* #1880) condemned those who thought that our Lord was not conceived in the womb of the blessed ever-virgin Mary from the Holy Spirit but rather from the seed of Joseph in the way other men are conceived (*sicut ceteros homines ex semine Joseph*). (e) See note 24 above.

[44] The citations in the previous note would be an eloquent proof of this. The shift of Christian focus is well documented by H. von Campenhausen, *The Virgin Birth in the Theology of the Ancient Church* (London: SCM, 1964).

Christians. And, while I welcome expert theological correction on this, I think that according to the usual criteria applied in Roman Catholic theology the virginal conception would be classified as a doctrine infallibly taught by the ordinary magisterium.

But here Catholics come to experience the type of anguish that fundamentalist Protestants have felt when biblical criticism has called into doubt their belief that the Bible is infallible (whether or not that term is used). If biblical criticism has qualified the notion of the inerrancy of the Bible, does modern historical study imply that the Roman Catholic notion of the infallibility of Church teaching also has to be qualified?

This question about the infallibility of Church teaching has two related aspects. *First,* is the whole notion of infallibility to be discarded or perhaps reduced to indefectibility? (The latter position would mean that while the Church may teach erroneously, it will never totally fail Christ.) This question has been answered affirmatively by Hans Küng in *Infallibility? An Inquiry.* The book is marred by its heated and counter-productive polemic against the Roman Curia. Moreover, as an illustration of a doctrine that was infallibly taught and subsequently called into doubt, Küng's choice of the Roman Church's teaching against artificial contraception is an unhappy one; for, as Karl Rahner has insisted, it is simply not clear that this teaching met all the requirements for a doctrine *de fide ex ordinario magisterio.* Nevertheless, when such weaknesses are acknowledged,[45] many theologians will admit that Küng has raised a question worthy of serious discussion. For instance, although in *The Survival of Dogma,* Avery Dulles does *not* agree with Küng that infallibility can be discarded or reduced to indefectibility (a point where I think Dulles is right), he does stress how conditioned the judgments of the teaching authority of the

---

[45] In the course of this book I shall on several occasions criticize views of Hans Küng. In light, however, of recent attacks on him, I feel obliged to insist that my differences from him are on a scholarly level and in no way would I ever impugn his stance as a dedicated Catholic. The German bishops in considering his book were very careful *not* to say it was heretical. More than one review, however, has pointed out its historical deficiencies.

Church are. Dulles speaks (p. 173) of "the historical relativity of all doctrinal statements." The doctrine of the virginal conception of Jesus would more clearly meet the usual criteria for being classified as infallible teaching than does Küng's example of artificial contraception. What would Dulles' thesis about "historical relativity" mean when applied to the historicity of the virginal conception?

Second, if we retain the possibility that the Church can teach infallibly, how valid are the criteria employed by theologians of the past in classifying doctrines as *de fide ex ordinario magisterio?* It is important to realize that precisely since this category involves doctrines that have not been explicitly defined by creed or by ecumenical council or by pope, it is the theologians who have made the classifying judgment as to which general Christian beliefs can be said to be infallible doctrines. Thus, in asking about the infallibility of the teaching concerning the virginal conception, we are not faced with the dilemma of whether an infallible teaching can suddenly become fallible. If one disagrees with Küng and accepts the possibility of infallibility, then logically if the virginal conception was taught infallibly in the past, it must remain an infallible teaching today (and tomorrow). The question that has arisen today is whether theologians were correct in their assumption that the virginal conception was universally and consistently proposed for belief by the Church *as an intrinsic constituent of divine revelation,* so that it was an infallible doctrine. As we have already suggested in the introduction,[46] a study of theological manuals over the last one hundred years suggests that the criteria used in judgments about infallibility are not easily applicable; for not only do theologians disagree among themselves on whether or not a doctrine is infallible, but also a doctrine commonly classified as infallible in one era of the manuals may no longer be so classified at a later period!

The application of the criteria of infallibility to the thesis of the virginal conception of Jesus is a particular problem precisely because this is a doctrine that has not been seriously

---

[46] See my remarks on infallibility and on evolution, pp. 8-9, 11-12.

challenged within Christianity until recent times. In patristic, medieval, and reformation times it was not the subject of a major dispute among Christians that would have forced the Church to come to a reflected decision on whether such a biological fact was intrinsically part of divine revelation. From *ca.* A.D. 200 to 1800 the virginal conception was attacked almost exclusively by those who denied Christianity in general or the divinity of Christ in particular. For the mass of Christians it was an unexamined doctrine taken for granted. As Jerome explained, "We believe that God was born of a virgin because we read it."[47] But now the virginal conception is being questioned by Christians who do not deny the divinity of Jesus —but who can no longer simply state with Jerome that they believe because they read it, since they now know the complexities of the scriptural accounts in which they read it. Are they automatically to be bound by the unreflective teaching of a past which was in no position to know the problems that must be faced now? Of course, it is almost axiomatic in Catholic theology that what the Church teaches does not draw its validity from the arguments used to reach that teaching, because the Church has an insight into revelation (through a type of spiritual connaturality) by which it transcends pure logic. But it is not clear how this principle applies to a question of biological *fact* such as is involved in the virginal conception. There is not much evidence that the Church had another chain of tradition back to the facts about Jesus' conception besides the affirmation common to Matthew and Luke. If that affirmation is called into question (as we shall see in Part V below), can one avoid seeing difficult implications for the Church's teaching on this subject?

Please understand: I am not saying that there is no longer impressive evidence for the virginal conception—personally I think that it is far more impressive than many who deny the virginal conception will admit. Nor am I saying that the Catholic position is dependent on the impressiveness of the scientifically controllable evidence, for I have just mentioned the

---

[47] *Adv. Helvidium* 19 (*PL* 23, 213A).

Catholic belief that the Holy Spirit can give to the Church a deeper perception than would be warranted by the evidence alone. I am simply asking whether for Catholics a modern evaluation of the evidence is irrelevant because the answer is already decided through past Church teaching. The very fact that theologians are discussing the limits of infallibility and how well the criteria for judging infallibility have been applied suggests that further investigation is not necessarily foreclosed.[48] As a help in any future study, I shall now survey as impartially as I can the doctrinal, historical, and biblical evidence pertinent to the virginal conception.

III. The Evidence from Interlocking Doctrines

We cannot consider the virginal conception of Jesus in isolation; it is related to other christological and mariological tenets that are dear to Christianity. Some of those tenets seem to favor the historicity of the virginal conception, while for other tenets the virginal conception is an obstacle. Let us consider both.

(A) Doctrines That Seemingly Suppose a Virginal Conception

(1) The sanctity of Mary.[49] All would recognize that, if

---

[48] In my personal opinion, for Roman Catholic Church authorities to seek to close this question by fiat and without discussion of the complexities of the evidence would be disastrous. Those of us who are loyal would obey, and the discussion will be left to those Catholics who ignore authority. A more likely reaction will be to dismiss the request for a serious re-examination as unthinkable. Pedagogically, such a response will scarcely satisfy a generation that constantly thinks the unthinkable. A serious re-examination, involving refined criteria for infallibility and a more critical approach to the biblical evidence, may well result in reaffirming that the virginal conception is truly of Christian faith; but then the very fact that we were willing to make an honest study will enhance the credibility of the position.

[49] I list the doctrines in an order of ascending importance. The mariological tenet is lowest in the scale because originally the vir-

there was a virginal conception, this involved an extraordinary intervention of God, so that Mary was truly the *kecharitōmenē* of Luke 1:28, the "favored one" of God. But the question raised here concerns more than the consequences of the use of God's miraculous power. There has existed in Christian thought the attitude, explicit or implicit, that virginal conception is a more noble way of conceiving a child than is marital intercourse; and this attitude is tied in to the thesis that virginity is the nobler form of Christian life. Most often in Christian literature this attitude was voiced not in immediate reference to Mary's virginal conception of Jesus but in reference to her remaining a virgin after Jesus' birth. Origen is the first major theologian to bring this ascetical motif to the fore: once overshadowed by the Holy Spirit, Mary could not conceivably have submitted to marital intercourse with a man. She thus becomes the model of all those who would choose virginity or celibacy as a way of life for the sake of the kingdom of God.[50]

Most modern theologians (including many Roman Catholics[51]) would not support an evaluation whereby the witness of

---

ginal conception was a christological concept, not a mariological one.

[50] Origen, *Comm. in Matt.* 10, 17 (*GCS* 40, 21). In *De institutione virginis* 5, 36 (PL 16, 328), Ambrose of Milan states, "By Mary's example all are summoned to the service [*cultus*] of virginity." Mary's virginity becomes one of the prominent reasons why God has so favored her. Pope Siricius, *Epistle* 9, 3 (*PL* 13, 1177), in the late fourth century, argues that if one denies the perpetual virginity, one plays into the hands of scoffers who say that Jesus could not have been born of a virgin.

[51] The Council of Trent (*DBS* #1810) stated, "If anyone says . . . that it is not better or holier to remain in virginity or celibacy than to be joined in marriage, let him be anathema." Yet, in the context of the sixteenth century, the real point of this was to defend the value of virginity against the attacks of some of the Reformers. The tendency among Roman Catholics today is not to compare virginity and marriage in terms of better or worse but to recognize that each has its uniqueness as a Christian witness. Because the choice of lifetime virginity for religious reasons is much less frequent than the choice of marriage, and because it is a choice that visibly renounces family continuity, the uniqueness of virginity is

Christian virginity is deemed simply as "better" than the witness of Christian married love. An anti-sexual bias that occasionally colored the theologizing of the past is not a dominant direction today. But there is an even more fundamental difficulty in linking the "greater" sanctity of virginity to the virginal conception, namely, that the infancy narratives do not make the slightest connection between the virginal conception and the special value of the state of virginity (a theme that *does* appear elsewhere in the NT, e.g., I Cor 7:8). Mary is depicted as having chosen the married state,[52] and the virginal conception is presented as God's intervention, not as Mary's personal choice. On the basis of the Gospel evidence it would be next to impossible to maintain that Mary would have been less holy if she had entered into normal marital relations with her husband and had borne Jesus through such relations.

(2) The sinlessness of Jesus. In Heb 4:15 Jesus is described as "one who has been tempted as we are in every respect, *yet*

---

often thought to be centered in the eschatological challenge it presents to the world.

[52] Few today interpret the "I do not know man" of Luke 1:34 as a vow or a resolve of virginity, *pace* G. Graystone, *Virgin of All Virgins* (Rome: Pio X, 1968). In the long run, as Graystone admits on pp. 147-51, the interpretation depends on whether Mary is to be considered a pious Jewish girl of her times (a situation that militates against a vow or resolve of virginity) or whether, by a special impulse of grace and in view of her future vocation, she broke out of the limitations of her surroundings and resolved to remain a virgin. Nevertheless, if most take the former alternative and think that Mary entered matrimony with the same intentions as any other girl, one cannot agree with Thomas Boslooper, *The Virgin Birth* (Philadelphia: Westminster, 1962), who uses Mary's choice to polemicize against what he deems a perverse Roman Catholic emphasis on virginity. On p. 235 he contends, "In the narrative of Jesus' birth a preview glimpse is given of the Savior's own teaching on sex and marriage. . . . Those who receive this story with faith accept premarital chastity, heterosexuality, and monogamous marriage as a divinely ordained way of life." This is an example of eisegesis (in an otherwise perceptive book). The infancy narratives are not meant to praise either marriage or virginity but the greatness of God's action.

without sinning," a description that Chalcedon (*DBS* #301) rephrased: "similar to us in all things *except sin.*" Ambrose and Augustine, the Fathers of the Western Church who figured prominently in developing the theology of original sin, explained that Jesus was free from sin because he was conceived of a virgin.[53] Behind this explanation lies the thesis that the transmission of original sin is bound up with the sexual nature of human propagation and the sensual appetites aroused by procreation. Many modern theologians feel an urgency to reformulate the truth contained in the doctrine of original sin, but even the defenders of the traditional understanding of the concept have for the most part abandoned the "concupiscence theory" of the propagation of sin. Thus, while the virginal conception may enter into the mystery of Jesus' sinlessness, it is difficult to argue that in order to be free from original sin Jesus had to be conceived of a virgin.[54]

(3) The divine sonship of Jesus. The vehemence of conservative Christian feeling with regard to the virginal conception may best be explained by the fact that in the past the denial of virginal conception has often been accompanied by a denial that Jesus is the Son of God. Nevertheless, historical Christianity has resisted attempts to identify incarnation with divine filiation in any sense that would have the deity as the male element unite with Mary as the female element to produce the human Son of God—in other words, a form of *hieros gamos.*[55]

---

[53] See the texts in Von Campenhausen, pp. 79-84. Thus the virginal conception becomes almost a theologoumenon of sinlessness. While the Greek Fathers did not deal with this matter in terms of original sin, they too related the moral perfection and sinlessness of Jesus to his virginal conception. Irenaeus, *Adv. Haer.* I, 30, 12 (*PG* 7, 702) seems to think of this as a Gnostic view; but see Hippolytus, *In Ps. xxii* (*GCS* 1², 146-47).

[54] K. Barth, *Church Dogmatics* 1² (Edinburgh: Clark, 1956), 188-92, makes a sophisticated connection between the lack of original sin and virginal conception. W. Pannenberg, *Jesus—God and Man* (Philadelphia: Westminster, 1968), p. 149, firmly disagrees with Barth.

[55] Of note is the Mormon belief that God the Father is human and corporeal (and masculine) in form—since we were created in

42 RAYMOND E. BROWN, S.S.

In A.D. 675, for instance, the Eleventh Council of Toledo (*DBS* #533) rejected the contention that, since Mary conceived by the overshadowing of the Holy Spirit, the Spirit was the father of Jesus. And so, while the doctrine of the virginal conception draws attention to the fact that Jesus was not simply a man like all others and is God's Son in a unique way, it would be impossible to prove theologically that the Son of God could not have become incarnate as the product of a marital union between Joseph and Mary. Both Protestant and Catholic theologians have stated clearly that the bodily fatherhood of Joseph would not have excluded the fatherhood of God.[56] Indeed, it is doubtful that if there had been no infancy narratives of Matthew and Luke (and thus there were no mention in the NT of the virginal conception), Christian faith in Jesus as God's Son would have been really different. The idea of divine sonship is substantiated in the Synoptic accounts of the baptism and the transfiguration, and in Pauline and Johannine christology; it is not dependent upon the infancy narratives.

(B) Doctrines Seemingly Unfavorable to a Virginal Conception

If theorizing about a natural conception does not seem to

His image and likeness—and that He begot His son of Mary.

[56] A conflict between the two fatherhoods was suggested by Tertullian, *Adv. Marcion* 4, 10 (*CSEL* 47, 446). It is rejected by P. Althaus, a Protestant theologian quoted with approval by Pannenberg (n. 54 above), p. 148, and by the Catholic theologian, J. Ratzinger, *Introduction to Christianity* (New York: Herder and Herder, 1969), p. 208. Ratzinger, who is relatively conservative, states: "According to the faith of the Church the Sonship of Jesus does not rest on the fact that Jesus had no human father: the doctrine of Jesus' divinity would not be affected if Jesus had been the product of a normal human marriage. For the Sonship of which faith speaks is not a biological but an ontological fact, an event not in time but in God's eternity." We may add that in the relationship between virginal conception and incarnation, it is not the first that is essential for the second; it is the second that makes the first credible.

raise insuperable difficulties in relation to the doctrines discussed above,[57] we may now ask the converse question: Does retention of the virginal conception raise insuperable difficulties for other Christian doctrines *as they are understood in our times*?

(1) Can the virginal conception be reconciled with the preexistence of the Son of God? Wolfhart Pannenberg has answered with a firm no: "In its content, the legend of Jesus' virgin birth stands in an irreconcilable contradiction to the Christology of the incarnation of the preexistent Son of God found in Paul and John."[58] His contention is based on the modern analysis of how NT christology developed. To simplify, we may say that NT christology developed backwards, from end to beginning.[59] The

---

[57] I speak, of course, on the level of logical conflicts. But man does not live by logic alone; and it may be that while there is no logical conflict between a natural conception of Jesus and these doctrines, *existentially* there is a conflict. For instance, abandoning the idea of a virginal conception, once it has been held, may very well have a deleterious impact on devotion to Mary and belief in the divinity of Jesus, despite the careful explanations of theologians. As I shall indicate in the conclusion to this chapter, I do not think such existential relationships can be discounted; but I am not clear on how decisive an argument they constitute in theology.

[58] Pannenberg (n. 54 above), p. 143. To discuss this question fully one would have to deal with sophisticated modern attempts to reinterpret pre-existence. See a Catholic attempt by P. Schoonenberg, *The Christ* (New York: Herder and Herder, 1971), pp. 80-91. In private correspondence H. Riesenfeld has suggested to me an argument that stands in direct contradiction to Pannenberg's thesis. According to Riesenfeld if one takes seriously the pre-existence of Christ *as a person,* then one has a real conflict in positing a natural generation. When a human being is begotten by a father and mother, a new personality comes into existence; but in classical Christian thought the conception of Jesus involved a pre-existent person. How this argument would fare in a theology that is non-Chalcedonian (as some modern theologies are tending to become) I shall have to leave to the systematic theologians to discuss. What is true is that a denial of the virginal conception has more often favored an adoptionist christology rather than a pre-existent christology.

[59] A full exposition may be found in R. H. Fuller, *The Founda-*

earliest Christians placed their "highest" christological emphasis
on the return of Jesus at the end of time, which was to come
shortly; it was then that he would be the Messiah and the Son
of Man (Acts 3:20-21). The next step was to realize that Jesus
had been exalted to a high christological status already at the
resurrection (Acts 2:36; 5:30-31), which (eventually) was
contrasted with a ministry of service and lowliness (Rom
1:3-4). As we see in the Gospel accounts of the public ministry,
the high christology was gradually moved back into the lifetime
of Jesus, so that he was the Messiah (Matt 16:16-17), the Son
of Man (Mark 8:31), and the Son of God (Mark 1:11; 9:7)
during the ministry.

Still a further step in Christian reflection was to push the
question back beyond the ministry and to ask at what earlier
stage he was all these things. In Matthew and Luke we have the
christology moved back to Jesus' infancy in Mary's womb, for an
angel proclaims that from the moment of his conception he was
already the Messiah and the Son of God. On the other hand,
in hymns quoted in the Pauline epistles (Philip 2:6-7; Col
1:15-17), in Hebrews (1:2), and in John (1:1; 17:5) the
christology is moved toward pre-existence. The NT authors did
not have the difficult task of reconciling these two "pre-ministry"
christologies, one centered on conception, the other on pre-
existence; for we have no evidence that the proponents of one
were aware of the other. But the later Church did reconcile
them by establishing a sequence whereby the pre-existent Word
or Son of God took flesh in the womb of the Virgin Mary and
became man.[60] Pannenberg rejects this reconciliation as false

tions of New Testament Christology (New York: Scribners, 1965)
and F. Hahn, The Titles of Jesus in Christology (Cleveland: World,
1969).

[60] The process is probably already at work in Ignatius of Antioch
who posits pre-existence for the divine element in Jesus who is conceived in the womb of Mary. (See A. Hoben, The Virgin Birth in
Historic and Linguistic Studies, second series, I [Chicago: Univ.,
1903], pp. 20-21.) Pre-existence and virginal conception are combined in Aristides, Apology 15, 1; and especially in Justin's writings
which speak of the virginal birth of the pre-existent Word (Apology
1, 21 and 33). In Melito's Discourse on Faith, 4 (Corpus Apolo-

because the original idea of the Matthean and Lucan infancy narratives was that Jesus first *became* God's Son through Mary's conception. He may well be right in his NT exegesis, but we have to ask why Matthew's and Luke's understanding of the christology of the virginal conception should be any more final than were the earlier NT understandings of the christology of the second coming or of that of the resurrection. Why is not the Church's reconciliation of pre-existence and virginal conception a genuine step in a developing christology? Because they are not reconciled in the NT does not mean, *pace* Pannenberg, that they are irreconcilable.[61]

(2) On the other side of the coin, can the virginal conception be reconciled with the true humanity of Jesus? Does Jesus become docetic if he was not conceived in a truly human manner? Is he a Jesus "similar to us in all things except sin?"[62] This question may well be unanswerable in the abstract, since we are dealing with something unique. We have said that Jesus would still have been God's Son if he had two human parents; how can we say that he would not be man's son if he had only one?[63] And, as we have seen, the *natus de virgine* was inserted into the creed with an anti-docetic purpose (n. 41 above).

Yet there is a very serious problem in reconciling the virginal conception with the modern understanding of how Jesus

---

getarum 9, 420), there is an attempted harmony between the Johannine Prologue and the infancy narratives.

[61] O. Piper, "The Virgin Birth: The Meaning of the Gospel Accounts," *Interpretation* 18 (1964), 132, states that if the virginal conception was once a rival to the Pauline and Johannine thesis of pre-existence, for the Church Fathers the virginal conception confirms pre-existence.

[62] Some have wondered if such a conception would not have made Jesus asexual, and they have related it to his remaining unmarried. This is another form of the connection made between virginal conception and lifetime virginity, a thesis rejected above when it was applied to Mary. Its application to Jesus goes back to Tertullian, *De carne Christi* 20 (*CSEL* 70, 241).

[63] Since the same evangelists who tell us about the virginal conception also give us genealogies of Jesus, they did not think that the conception ruptured the chain of human descent.

functioned as a human being who was limited in the way he could *express or formulate* his own identity[64]—a Jesus who did not speak of himself as "Messiah," as "Son of God," and perhaps not even as "Son of Man." The history of christology given above assumes that "high" explicit christology was the contribution and insight of the Christian community, while the christology of Jesus' lifetime was implicit, i.e., implied in his words and actions but not expressed in titles. However, if Joseph and Mary knew that their son had no human father but was begotten of God's holy spirit, if it had been revealed to them from the start that the child was to be the Messiah, and if they had not kept this secret from Jesus, how can he *not* have affirmed that he was the Messiah or that he was the unique Son of God? Obviously this conflict between the infancy narratives and the (reconstructed) Jesus of the ministry is based on many "ifs," all of which can be questioned.[65]

One may even argue forcefully in the opposite direction. The historical Jesus came to his ministry with an assurance that he could tell men what God wanted of them (as implied in his very proclamation of the kingdom and in his use of the initial, authoritative "Amen") and that he could act with God's power (the exorcisms). What was the source of this assurance, which involved some kind of awareness of his own identity? Was the source his knowledge that he had no human father

---

[64] In my book *Jesus God and Man* (Milwaukee: Bruce, 1967), pp. 92-93, I acknowledged that the limitations of Jesus' knowledge of himself, traceable in the Synoptic picture of the ministry, were not reconcilable with the pictures of Jesus offered by the Fourth Gospel and the infancy narratives. The fourth evangelist has re-written the story of the ministry in light of late first-century christology, so that Jesus speaks as the pre-existent Son who was with the Father before creation. Matthew and Luke have not so totally re-written the story of the ministry, but they have created a tension between the implications of the ministry and what is explicit in the infancy narratives.

[65] Perhaps, for instance, the direct divine intervention in the conception of the child would still have been interpreted in the OT light of God's adoptive fatherhood toward the Davidic kings, and not in terms of ontological fatherhood.

and thus was uniquely God's Son? The latter might explain his strange custom of addressing God intimately as *"Abba."* Yet there remains the difficulty that such a specific knowledge of his origins did not result in an ability to formulate his role in christological titles (e.g., the titles given to him in the annunciation of his birth) or in clearer descriptions.

In summary of the evidence from interlocking doctrines, we note that the balance seems to be shifting from an almost perfect harmony of the virginal conception with other mariological and christological tenets to disturbing difficulties about its reconcilability with some thrusts of modern christological insights.

IV. The Evidence from Early History

By the year A.D. 200 the virginal conception of Jesus was "in possession" as a Christian doctrine. Formerly the claim might have been made that this was already true by A.D. 100 since Ignatius of Antioch mentions the virginal conception in his letters.[66] Yet Walter Bauer's *Orthodoxy and Heresy in Early Christianity* (German ed. 1934) has forcefully reminded us that the second century was not a uniform or homogeneous period in Christian thought, for what was accepted in one area was rejected or unknown in another, and what triumphed as orthodoxy at the end of the century was often but one competing idea earlier. On the one hand, then, we may ask if large groups of Christians betrayed ignorance of the virginal conception during the second century. And were there Christians who did not accept the virginal conception and whose rejection of it is indicative of a historical tradition that knew of a natural conception of Jesus? On the other hand, we may search for evidence of Christian belief that came from non-canonical sources and which might supplement the testimony of the infancy narratives.[67]

---

[66] In *Ephesians* 7:2; 18:2; 19:1; *Smyrnaeans* 1:1.

[67] Of particular help here are the excellent surveys of historical evidence by Hoben (n. 60 above) and Von Campenhausen (n. 44 above). I would judge the latter a bit minimalistic (e.g., n. 76

First, the rejection of the virginal conception. Two groups are involved: Gnostics and Jewish Christians. In the gnostic or sectarian camp the names of Cerdo, Cerinthus, Satornilus, the Carpocratians, Marcion, and the Manicheans may be mentioned. Of them Von Campenhausen[68] says, "We must not regard these views as entirely secondary and directed against the doctrine of the virgin birth; they are, on the contrary, further evidence of how little the virgin birth was taken as a matter of course, even at the beginning and up to the middle of the second century." That may be true and of importance for evaluating whether the virginal conception was believed *ubique, semper, et ab omnibus;* but the variant views of most of these groups tell us little about the possible historical validity of a contrary tradition. Often their opposition to the virginal conception stems from doctrinal or philosophical presuppositions (docetism, disdain for the worldly, etc.) rather than from historical reasons. One can scarcely take seriously their alternative explanations of Jesus' origins, e.g., Marcion's seeming contention that a supernatural being came down directly from heaven in the fifteenth year of Tiberius, at the time of Jesus' baptism by John.[69]

Much more important is the rejection of the virginal conception by Jewish Christians. In mid-second century Justin,[70] who

---

below), in part because he does not give sufficient attention to the apocrypha (pseudepigrapha) as evidence of early Christian belief.

[68] *Op cit.,* p. 22; see also Hoben, *op. cit.,* pp. 33-55.

[69] Some of the other views listed by Von Campenhausen, *op. cit.,* p. 22[1], are that the Holy Spirit was Jesus' mother, that Mary was an angel, that Jesus was the angel Gabriel or Michael who entered into Mary to take on human form. On the other hand, Cerinthus, the Carpocratians, and the *Acts of Thomas* agree with the Jewish Christian evidence in asserting that Jesus was the natural son of Joseph.

[70] *Trypho* 48, 4 (reading "your race" rather than "our race" as in *PG* 6, 581). Justin's tone seems to indicate that these Jewish Christians were not considered out-and-out heretics (Von Campenhausen, *op. cit.,* p. 22), but by the end of the century and the time of Irenaeus (*Adv. Haer.* III 19, 1; *Sources Chrétiennes* 34, 330) there was much less fluidity about the obligation to accept the virginal conception.

himself believed that Jesus was conceived of a virgin, acknowledged the existence of Jews who accepted Jesus as the Messiah but declared that he was of merely human origin. Somewhat later Origen[71] knew of the Ebionites or Jews who had accepted Jesus as the Messiah; and he reported, "There are two sects of Ebionites: the one confessing as we do that Jesus was born of a virgin, the other holding that he was not born in this way but like other men." Considering the relationship of both Justin and Origen to Palestine, we may wonder if these Jewish Christians preserved a tradition that had come down in that country from some of the original followers of Jesus who knew nothing of his having been conceived of a virgin and thought that he was Joseph's natural son. Some recent evidence, but of very dubious value,[72] may be cited in favor of that view. On the other hand, as we shall see below, there are Christian works of Jewish background that show early acceptance of the virginal conception.

Second, how widely was the virginal conception known? It has often been noted that of "the Apostolic Fathers" only Ignatius of Antioch makes reference to the virginal conception, and

---

[71] *Contra Celsum* 2, 1 and 5, 61 (*GCS* 2, 126-27 and 3, 65).

[72] I refer to the material published by Shlomo Pines, *The Jewish Christians of the Early Centuries of Christianity according to a New Source* (Proceedings of the Israel Academy of Sciences and Humanities, II, no. 13; Jerusalem: Central Press, 1966). Behind an Arabic, tenth-century Moslem polemic against Christians, Pines detects a fifth-century Syriac account of Nazarene or Jewish Christian beliefs. The document claims that this sect was driven out of Palestine into Syria around A.D. 62. These Jewish Christians believed that Jesus was "the son of Joseph the Carpenter," as opposed to being one "born without [fecundation by] a male" (66b; Pines, p. 45). However, the lateness and nature of the evidence create serious doubts about its reliability, especially in regard to first-century Palestinian Christianity. The author seems to know both the Matthean and Lucan infancy traditions; e.g., he reports that Joseph took the child and his mother to Egypt and that Joseph and Mary searched for the lost child in Jerusalem (94b; Pines, p. 51). The tradition that Jesus was the son of Joseph may reflect the Sinaiticus Syriac variant of Matt 1:16 (rather than Matt 1:1 to which Pines, p. 8, refers), in combination with Matt 13:55.

many think that this silence is not a matter of chance. Von Campenhausen,[73] for instance, thinks the silence is especially significant on the part of the *Letter of Barnabas* and the *Shepherd of Hermas* since both of these works have speculation about the Lord's origins. While that may be,[74] there is a surprising amount of evidence that the virginal conception was known and accepted during the second century by Christians of various origins and many places.

Let us begin with Ignatius of Antioch who associates the virginity of Mary with the birth and death of Jesus as "three resounding mysteries wrought in the silence of God" (*Ephesians* 19:1). The association with other doctrines that he makes and the assurance with which he makes it would indicate Ignatius could take for granted the acceptance of Mary's virginity. Since it is scarcely by exclusive choice that he mentions it only in *Ephesians* and *Smyrnaeans,* we may assume that the virginity of Mary would have been known by all or most of the (largely Gentile) congregations whom he addresses in Asia Minor and Rome, and also at Antioch (a church with deep Jewish roots) where he was bishop. We are not certain whether Ignatius draws upon the canonical Matthean infancy narrative or upon independent tradition[75]—if the latter, his witness would be even more important. A few years later (*ca.* 125) Aristides of Athens refers to the Son of God taking flesh of a virgin.[76] Knowledge of the virginal conception among the apologists is also attested in the writings of Justin (mid-second century), whose witness

---

[73] *Op. cit.,* p. 19.

[74] The virginal conception would not be harmonious with the theology of the author of *Barnabas* who understood Jesus to be Son of God in a way that was irreconcilable with his being son of David (12:10).

[75] Boslooper, (n. 52 above), p. 28, argues for this.

[76] Von Campenhausen, *op. cit.,* p. 19[4], rightly points out glosses in the text of Aristides' *Apology* 15, 1, which can be determined by comparing the Greek and the Syriac; but I wonder does the reader come away from Von Campenhausen's note with *the fact* clearly in mind that there is a reference to incarnation "of a virgin" in all three forms of Aristides' work (Armenian, Greek, Syriac).

is important because he came from Palestine and may have preserved some Palestinian non-canonical material about Jesus' birth.[77] Elsewhere in the Gentile Christian world of the second century the virginal conception is supported by Tatian, Abercius of Hierapolis, Melito of Sardis, the Old Roman Creed, and the *Protevangelium of James.*[78] Among Christians of peculiarly Semitic interests or background we have the witness of the *Testaments of the Patriarchs*[79] and the *Ascension of Isaiah.*[80] Of particular importance is the witness to a virginal conception in the *Odes of Solomon,* because of the efforts of James Charlesworth to establish that this is a *first-century* Jewish Christian work, not dependent on the canonical infancy narratives.[81]

---

[77] See E. F. Bishop, *Evangelical Quarterly* 39 (1967), 30-39. Nevertheless, while Justin knew Jewish views and made considerable use of OT prophecies in defending the virginal conception (*Apology* 1, 33; *Trypho* 77-78 and 84), his personal outlook and exegesis was that of a Gentile Christian.

[78] Although this apocryphal gospel pretends to come from Jesus' family circle (his step-brother James), the author was not a Palestinian Jew, for he betrays real ignorance of the Temple and its customs. Writing in mid-second century, he combines the Matthean and Lucan information with imaginative details of another origin.

[79] *Joseph* 19:8 mentions the spotless lamb born of a virgin. While scholars are not agreed whether this is a pre-Christian Jewish document with Christian interpolations (R. H. Charles) or an original Jewish Christian compilation (M. de Jonge), most would see here a testimony to the virginal conception coming from the second century at the latest. On the *Testaments* see A.-M. Denis, *Introduction aux pseudépigraphes grecs d'Ancien Testament* (Leiden: Brill, 1970), pp. 49-59.

[80] The apocalyptic "Vision of Isaiah," which constitutes the second half of the *Ascension,* is generally attributed to Jewish Christian circles of the late first or early second centuries. The author of the "Vision" knows Matthew's Gospel. See E. Hennecke and W. Schneemelcher, *New Testament Apocrypha* II (Philadelphia: Westminster, 1965), 642-44; also J. Daniélou, *The Theology of Jewish Christianity* (Chicago: Regnery, 1964), pp. 12-14.

[81] *Ode* 19:6-9. For Charlesworth's articles see *Catholic Biblical Quarterly* 31 (1969), 357-69; *Semitics* 1 (1970), 12-26; *Revue Biblique* 77 (1970), 522-49. By courtesy he permitted me to use his translation in the forthcoming *The Odes of Solomon* (Oxford:

In summary, then, the over-all picture from the early historical evidence is one of reasonably wide affirmation for the virginal conception. Yet there are some puzzling instances of silence that may indicate ignorance or rejection, along with explicit rejection in certain Jewish Christian circles, raising the possibility (but no more than that) of a contrary historical tradition in favor of human fatherhood. Certainly, therefore, the problem cannot be settled on the basis of the early historical evidence, for that evidence does not drastically erode support for the virginal conception, as some have claimed.

V. The Evidence from the Scriptures

Since our other forms of evidence ultimately refer back to the infancy narratives of Matthew and Luke, the value of the scriptural evidence for the virginal conception will have a great effect on any ultimate decision about historicity. The scope of this discussion requires that I treat the NT with the same brevity with which I scanned the other areas. And so I shall leave to a future book a full treatment of the infancy narratives[82] and attempt here only to list factors on both sides of the question of historicity, warning the readers that I cannot do justice to all the subtleties. But first let me summarize in a few sentences the place of the virginal conception within the infancy narratives. It seems clear that the two evangelists traditionally known as Matthew and Luke, writing in the era A.D. 80-100, believed that, in conceiving Jesus, Mary remained bodily a virgin and

Clarendon, 1973). However, we should note that in the *Odes* the virginal conception is associated with the thesis of a feminine Holy Spirit and a painless birth—ideas known to us in Christian circles of the *second* century, the date more commonly assigned to the *Odes*. The thesis that *Ode* 19 is a later insertion has been generally abandoned.

[82] Although modern Protestant and Catholic scholars are in surprising agreement on the generally figurative and non-historical character of the infancy narratives, there really is no adequate commentary on these Gospel chapters in English. Much of the excellent foreign Catholic work has had little impact in America.

did not have intercourse with Joseph (see note 37 above)—
they were not consciously presenting us with a theologoumenon.
Neither evangelist knew the other's infancy narrative, and the
fact that a virginal conception through the power of the Holy
Spirit is one of the few points on which they agree means that
this tradition antedated both accounts. Indeed, it had been in circulation long enough to have developed into (or to have been
employed in) narratives of a quite diverse character and to
have circulated in different Christian communities. Now we
must ask whether this common tradition was historical in its
origins.

(A) Scriptural Arguments Against Historicity

(1) The "high" christology implied in a virginal conception.
The most serious objection to historicity has already been mentioned at the end of Section III. The explicit and high christology of the infancy narratives centering on the virginal conception
is hard to reconcile with the widely accepted critical theory of
a gradual development of explicit NT christology, unless the
virginal conception is considered to be a late christological
theologoumenon. If the christology associated with virginal conception was known from the first moments of Jesus' earthly
career, the whole critical theory falls apart. This difficulty is
not insuperable if scholars can work out a distinction between
the fact of virginal conception and *the christology* that surrounds
it in the infancy narratives, but that has not yet been done in a
satisfactory way. Further investigation in this direction is im-
perative if we are to resolve the principal modern objection to
the virginal conception.

(2) The dubious historicity of the infancy material in general. I have already pointed out at the beginning of Section II
that we know little of the sources from which the various infancy
traditions were drawn and thus the infancy narratives differ
from the rest of the Gospels. But our problems deepen when
we compare the two infancy narratives, one to the other; for,
despite ingenious attempts at harmonization, the basic stories

are virtually irreconcilable (cf. Matt 2:14 and Luke 2:39). They agree in so few details that we may say with certainty that they cannot both be historical *in toto*. Even the lists of Jesus' ancestors that they give are very different, and neither one is plausible.[83]

If we consider them separately, Matthew's account is redolent of the folkloric and imaginative: e.g., angelic appearances in dreams, guiding birth star, treasures from the East, the machinations of a wicked king, the slaughter of innocent children.[84] Luke's account has less of the folkloric, even though it reports several angelic appearances and a miraculous punishment of Zechariah. Yet Luke shows signs of considerable literary artistry and organization; e.g., a delicate balance between two annunciations and two births, joined by the visitation—obviously this is not the atmosphere of purely historical reporting. Moreover, some of the Lucan details are of dubious historicity, namely, a family relationship between the Baptist and Jesus;[85] or a census of the Roman world that affected Galilee and occurred before the death of Herod the Great.[86]

Once again the difficulty is not insuperable. Most scholars

[83] The Matthean genealogy with its three groupings of fourteen generations is obviously artificial; it contains well-known confusions in the first two groupings and is impossibly short for the third or post-exilic period; moreover, it records a priestly name like Zadok which is not expected in a Davidic list. The Lucan genealogy also follows a numerical pattern (probably 77 names) and may have duplications (compare 3:23-24 to 3:29-30); it attributes names of a definite post-exilic type to the pre-exilic period.

[84] While the raw material is folkloric, the accounts are remarkably brief; they have been pruned down to the bare storyline and to suit the evangelist's pedagogical interests in OT fulfillment. See the analysis by A. Vögtle, *Bibel und Leben* 6 (1965), 246-79, especially 263-65.

[85] Such a relationship could not even be suspected from any other NT evidence and certainly was not known by the fourth evangelist (John 1:31).

[86] See the superb summary of the evidence by G. Ogg, "The Quirinius Question Today," *Expository Times* 79 (1967-68), 231-36, who shows how difficult it is to avoid the conclusion that Luke has confused the dating of the Roman census.

today would agree that each infancy narrative is composite: information or stories from different sources have been combined and edited by the two evangelists. Thus it is possible that some of the sources wore folkloric or non-historical, while other sources or items of tradition came down from genuine family memories. Virginal conception through the power of the Holy Spirit could have been in the latter category, precisely because it is common to the two evangelists. Nevertheless, one must admit that the general context of the infancy narratives, in which the virginal conception is preserved, does nothing to increase our confidence in historicity.

A particular difficulty should be mentioned. The virginal conception is intimately (but perhaps not inextricably) associated with the Davidic descent of Jesus and his birth at Bethlehem, two affirmations that are also often considered as theologoumena by modern biblical criticism. It is suggested that because the early Christians confessed Jesus as Messiah, for which "Son of David" was an alternative title, they historicized their faith by creating for him Davidic genealogies and by claiming that Joseph was a Davidide.[87] Similarly, the theory continues,

---

[87] The latest full-scale discussion is that by C. Burger, *Jesus als Davidssohn* (FRLANT 98; Göttingen, Vandenhoeck, 1970) who doubts that the thesis of Davidic descent can be traced back to the Semitic-speaking Christian circles of Palestine; it is a product of Hellenistic Jewish Christianity. But Burger does not really solve the objection to his thesis raised by the fact that James, the brother of the Lord, was known widely in the Christian world and lived into the 60's. The popular thesis of his "brother's" Davidic descent must have circulated in James' lifetime and could scarcely not have reached his ears. Can we posit James' acquiescence in such a fictional affirmation about the family ancestry? Would not others who knew the family and, especially, the Jewish opponents have raised some objection? Paul makes his own a creedal statement about Jesus' Davidic descent (Rom 1:3); he knew James and he was scarcely indifferent about questions of family origin (Rom 11:1; Philip 3:5). As for the oft-cited Mark 12:35-37a (which Bultmann does not consider historical), it need not be interpreted as a rhetorical question implying a negation of Davidic sonship. Rather it may be a rabbinic *haggada*-type question requiring that two seemingly contradictory scriptural positions be reconciled—the Messiah is both

they localized his birth in the Davidic birthplace of Bethlehem.[88] The probative value of the arguments for this theory is debatable, as I have indicated in the notes; but once again the virginal conception is surrounded by the dubious.

(3) The silence of the rest of the NT. The questionable historical character of the infancy narratives makes the silence of the rest of the NT about the virginal conception all the more significant. The NT material that rests in some way on apostolic witness (Pauline letters; Gospel traditions of the ministry) offers no support for the virginal conception; indeed not even all the infancy traditions support it. Let us try to evaluate the silence in each instance as to whether it implies ignorance or rejection of the virginal conception.

Paul. The Pauline letters are the earliest Christian writings; yet their problem-oriented character makes it very difficult to judge if Paul's silence on this question is accidental or signifi-

---

David's Son and David's Lord, but in different ways. See D. Daube, *The New Testament and Rabbinic Judaism* (London: Athlone, 1956), pp. 158-69.

[88] Unlike Davidic descent, birth at Bethlehem is attested only in the infancy narratives; but since it appears in both, it is an antecedent datum. Again Burger, p. 104, is too negative; "The overwhelming evidence to the contrary has made the thesis that Bethlehem was *not* the historical birthplace of Jesus the *communis opinio* of NT scholarship." While there was an expectation of the Messiah's birth at Bethlehem (Matt 2:4-6; John 7:42), there were other Jewish views of the Messiah's origin to which Christians might have appealed if Jesus were not born at Bethlehem (see John 7:27); and certainly Jesus was hailed as Messiah when he was known only as Jesus *of Nazareth.* As for the rest of the NT evidence, it is not certain that John 7:41-42 represents the evangelist's ignorance or denial of birth at Bethlehem, for it may be an instance of irony— cf. John 4:12 where the evangelist and the reader, but not the speaker, know the true situation. (Yet John does portray Jesus' contemporaries as ignorant of his birth at Bethlehem.) A greater problem is Mark 6:1-3 where family acquaintances at Nazareth (called Jesus' "native region") betray no knowledge of Jesus' having been born elsewhere and, in particular, of his having been born in the town of David which might have been auspicious of his present fame.

cant.[89] That Paul described Jesus as "born of a woman" (Gal 4:4) rather than as "born of a virgin" is scarcely probative;[90] and his reference to Jesus as the "seed of David" (Rom 1:3) and the "seed of Abraham" (Gal 3:16) is no more specific in its information about the "how" of Jesus' conception than is Matthew's description (1:1) of Jesus as "son of David, son of Abraham," a description that Matthew found reconcilable with virginal conception. More important is the tension already mentioned (p. 44 above) between the pre-existence motif in hymns cited by Paul and the christology of virginal conception. On the other hand, scholars[91] have detected close vocabulary parallels between Rom 1:3-4 and Luke 1:31-35, indicating a possible relation between a Pauline creedal formula and the Lucan tradition of virginal conception. Ultimately, however, there seems to be no way to establish persuasively whether or not Paul knew of the virginal conception.

Mark. The virginal conception is not mentioned by the earliest Gospel, which paradoxically, however, is the only Gospel that does *not* refer to Jesus as the "son of Joseph" or the "son of the carpenter."[92] (Indeed, as we shall see,[93] it is

---

[89] To argue that, if Paul knew of the virginal conception, he would have mentioned it in the course of his observations on virginity is to make an unwarranted connection between virginal conception and virginity as a life-style, a connection never made in the NT.

[90] Indeed an argument *for* the virginal conception has been based on Paul's phrase "born of a woman." It has been pointed out that in Gal 4 Paul uses "born" (*genomenon;* also Rom 1:3; Philip 2:7) in refering to Jesus' origins but "begotten" (*gegennētai* or *gennē-theis*) in referring to the origins of Ishmael and Isaac. See W. C. Robinson, "A Re-study of the Virgin Birth of Christ," *Evangelical Quarterly* 37 (Oct.-Dec. 1965), published as a *Supplement to the Columbia Theological Seminary Bulletin* (1966), pp. 1-14.

[91] J. Orr, *The Virgin Birth of Christ* (New York: Scribners, 1907), pp. 120-21; G. A. Danell, *Studia Theologica* 4 (1950), 94-101. This argument is independent of the unverifiable assumption that Luke, Paul's companion, was the evangelist, an assumption that vitiates much of R. J. Cooke's *Did Paul Know of the Virgin Birth?* (New York: Macmillan, 1926).

[92] These designations are found in Matthew (13:55) and in Luke

significant that Mark refers to Jesus as "son of *Mary*.") Some
interpreters deem the omission of an infancy narrative sufficient
proof that Mark knew nothing about Jesus' birth. Yet, in Mark's
time would a birth tradition, even if well known, have already
been considered part of the public proclamation of the Good
News and hence something in the category of Gospel? Others
point out that Marcan christology is not so "high" as that of
the infancy narratives. For instance, in Mark 8:29-30 Jesus
reacts against a confession that he is the Messiah. But the same
reaction is found in Luke 9:20-21, a Gospel that has an infancy
narrative where we are told that Jesus is the Messiah.[94] If
Mark's account of the baptism of Jesus (1:11) *can* be interpreted as an adoption of Jesus as God's Son at that moment
(probably a wrong interpretation) and thus as a negation of the
christology of the infancy narratives, so can Luke's account of
the baptism[95]—and Luke *did* accept the christology of the infancy narratives. Exegetes who join Mark 3:21 to 3:31-35

(five times), evangelists who clearly believe in the virginal conception; and thus they need imply no more than Joseph's legal or
"public" paternity. Of course, they may have been taken over by
Matthew and Luke from an earlier usage where there was no
knowledge of virginal conception; yet it remains true that the designations themselves tell us nothing about the user's attitude on this
question. It is striking that Mark 6:3, if we accept the best textual
witnesses, refers to Jesus as "the carpenter," while Matt 13:55 refers
to him as "the carpenter's son." If the usage were the reverse, there
would be exegetical unanimity that "the carpenter's son" in Mark
(implying Joseph's natural fatherhood) was the original reading,
changed by Matthew to "the carpenter" to favor virginal conception. Unfortunately, facts get in the way of theory.

[93] See n. 115 below and the discussion pertinent to it.

[94] There is an unreconciled conflict in Luke between the two
christologies (of the ministry and of the infancy), as we have previously insisted; but the fact that they can coexist in Luke makes it
difficult to be sure what Mark's attitude would have been.

[95] Indeed, more so if one accepts the Western reading of Luke
3:22: "You are my Son; *today* I have begotten you"—a reading,
however, that may be just a later scribal "improvement," smoothing
out a mixed citation (Ps 2:7 and Isa 42:1), in favor of citing only
Ps 2:7.

would have Jesus' "mother and brothers" (3:31) thinking that Jesus was "out of his mind" (3:21)—an attitude scarcely reconcilable with Mary's knowledge of the uniqueness of her son's conception—but the relation of the two texts is not lucidly clear in Mark. In general, then, Marcan silence may well mean Marcan ignorance of the virginal conception, but the evidence leaves much to be desired.

John. The last of the Gospels is also silent on the virginal conception. The third-person singular reading in John 1:13: *"He who* was begotten, not by blood, nor by carnal desire, nor by man's desire, but of God," is considered by most[96] an early patristic change from the original plural in order to make the text christologically useful. Jesus is called "son of Joseph" in John 1:45 and 6:42 (but see n. 92). Some would find John's ignorance of the virginal conception made more likely by his seeming ignorance of Jesus' birth at Bethlehem (John 7:42; but see n. 88). On p. 44 above I have already explained that a tension exists between John's thesis of Jesus' pre-existence and the christological direction taken by the infancy narratives. Overall, the scales tip in favor of Johannine ignorance of the virginal conception; and that means the ignorance of it in a late-first-century Christian community that had access to an early tradition about Jesus.[97] On the other hand, some suggest that the Fourth Gospel stems from the region of Antioch; and it is interesting that less than twenty years after the Gospel's composition, Ignatius, the bishop of Antioch who reflects certain Johannine ideas (whether or not he knew the Gospel), was firmly convinced of the virgin birth.

Sections of the infancy narratives. We have already stated that the infancy narratives are probably composite, an amalga-

---

[96] Although not found in a single Greek Gospel ms., this reading is still accepted by a surprising number of French-speaking exegetes: M.-E. Boismard, F.-M. Braun, D. Mollat (in the "Bible of Jerusalem"), and exhaustively defended by J. Galot, *Etre né de Dieu: Jean 1:13* (*Analecta Biblica* 37; Rome: Pontifical Biblical Institute, 1969).

[97] This is the least one can conclude from C. H. Dodd, *Historical Tradition in the Fourth Gospel* (Cambridge University, 1963).

mation of different traditions. It is very likely that certain of these traditions were composed in ignorance of a virginal conception. As for Luke, most scholars have given up the thesis that Luke 1:34-35, which contains the only clear reference in this infancy narrative to virginal conception, is a post-Lucan scribal addition.[98] Yet there is considerable agreement that chapter 2 of Luke may have come from a tradition independent of 1:34-35 and ignorant of a virginal conception.[99] Certainly Mary's puzzlement in 2:48-49 is explained more easily on this supposition. Also the modifying phrase in Luke 3:23 ("Jesus being the son, *as was supposed,* of Joseph, the son of Heli. . . .") may be Luke's correction of a genealogy that originally listed Jesus as the natural son of Joseph. As for Matthew, there is reason to detect an underlying story involving a series of angelic visions to Joseph, in which the first vision may have originally announced only the birth of the child Savior, and not his virginal conception.[100] Personally, I find Matthew's genealogy of less significance than Luke's, since I think that Matthew added the names of Joseph and Jesus to an already existing popular genealogy of the Messiah king, and therefore there was no

---

[98] V. Taylor, *The Historical Evidence for the Virgin Birth* (Oxford: Clarendon, 1920), pp. 40-80, argues that the verses are Lucan but added as an afterthought. Yet their presence parallels 1:18ff. in the annunciation of the Baptist's birth and seems integral to the chapter. See J. G. Machen, *The Virgin Birth of Christ* (New York: Harper, 1930), pp. 120-53.

[99] M. Dibelius, *From Tradition to Gospel* (New York: Scribners, 1935), pp. 123-27; R. Leaney, *New Testament Studies* 8 (1961-62), 158-63. Acceptance of this point does not necessarily involve acceptance of Dibelius' thesis about the non-historical origins of the theme of virginal conception. See the very careful discussion and refutation of Dibelius' thesis by Grelot (n. 29 above).

[100] C. T. Davis, "Tradition and Redaction in Matthew 1:18—2-23," *Journal of Biblical Literature* 90 (1971), 404-21. Independently, I reached almost the same conclusions about the story underlying Matthew on the basis of other evidence, namely, the Jewish midrash on the birth of Moses on which the pre-Matthean story was patterned and which does not involve a virginal conception. I disagree with Davis on whether the pregnancy-divorce motif was so prominent in the pre-Matthean story.

previous attitude in the genealogy toward Jesus as the son of Joseph.[101]

As a summary reflection on the silence of these various NT documents in relation to the virginal conception, I would have to insist that, even when this silence indicates ignorance, it does not disprove the historicity of the virginal conception. Such a conception would not have been part of the early proclamation, for it opened Jesus' origins to ridicule and calumny. One might theorize, then, that a family tradition about the virginal conception circulated among relatively few in the period A.D. 30-60 before it spread and became known by communities such as those for whom Matthew and Luke wrote. On the other hand, the silence of the rest of the NT enhances the *possibility* of the theologoumenon theory whereby sometime in the 60's one or more Christian thinkers solved the christological problem by affirming symbolically that Jesus was God's Son from the moment of his conception. According to the theory, they used an imagery of virginal conception whose symbolic origins were forgotten as it was disseminated among various Christian communities and recorded by the evangelists.

(B) Scriptural Arguments Favoring Historicity

The evidence is not one-sided and the theologoumenon theory leaves at least two knotty problems unsolved.

(1) The origins of the idea of a *virginal* conception. It is well attested that tales of marvelous births are created posthumously for great men, especially religious leaders; this is a way of showing that Providence had selected these men from the beginning. Undoubtedly, such a tendency influenced the formation of the infancy stories concerning Jesus; but our immediate concern is whether such a process explains one precise point: the Christian contention that Jesus was conceived virginally. If the Christian narrative of the conception of Jesus were

---

[101] Most scholars do not accept as original the Sinaiticus Syriac reading of Matt 1:16 which makes Joseph the (natural?) father of Jesus.

like the Lucan story (1:5-20) of how the Baptist was conceived, namely, through divine assistance that made aged and barren parents fertile, there would be little difficulty in accepting the theologoumenon theory—the conception could be explained as a symbolic, theological construction imitating similar birth narratives in the OT, e.g., of Isaac and of Samuel. But the story of Jesus' conception has, in fact, taken a form for which, to the best of our knowledge, there is no exact parallel or antecedent in the material available to the Christians of the first century who told of this conception.

The wealth of comparative material almost defies summary.[102] Without sufficient concern as to whether they would have been known by or acceptable to early Christians, *non-Jewish parallels* have been found in the figures of world religions (the births of the Buddha, Krishna, and the son of Zoroaster), in Greco-Roman mythology, in the births of the Pharaohs (with the god Amun-Ra acting through the father)[103] and in the marvelous births of emperors and philosophers (Augustus, Plato, etc.). But these "parallels" consistently involve a type of *hieros gamos* where a divine male, in human or other form, impregnates a woman, either through normal sexual intercourse or through some substitute form of penetration. They are not really similar to the non-sexual virginal conception that is at the core of the infancy narratives, a conception where there is no male deity or element to impregnate Mary.[104]

---

[102] A competent survey is provided by Boslooper (n. 52 above), pp. 135-86.

[103] This is stressed as an antecedent for the Christian stories by E. Brunner-Traut, *Zeitschrift für Religions-und Geistesgeschichte* 12 (1960), 99-111. But the best parallels she offers are to the general (and often folkloric) details of the infancy narratives, and she does not resolve the main difficulty that the Pharaohs were thought to have been conceived by intercourse.

[104] Let me call attention to a few seeming exceptions: (a) Plutarch, *Life of Numa*, 4: "The Egyptians believe, not implausibly, that it is not impossible for the spirit of a god to approach a woman and procure in her certain beginnings of parturition." Yet he argues that it ought to work the other way around and that a man ought to be able *to have intercourse* with a goddess. (b) Aeschylus,

More logically others have turned to seek parallels in the Jewish background. In pre-Christian *Hebrew or Aramaic sources,* however, no expectation or description of virginal conception has yet been found, even in reference to the coming Messiah.[105] The allusion to a divine begetting of the Messiah or Anointed One that appears in the Qumran documents[106] involves no more than the divine adoptive begetting (coronation) of the anointed king in the royal psalms (Ps 2:7).

Hellenistic Judaism has seemed a more fertile field for

Suppliants, vv. 17-19, speaks of Zeus making Io a mother "with a mystic breath" (which could be interpreted as spirit). But a few lines on we hear that Io was "quickened with Zeus' veritable *seed,*" and Hera becomes jealous. (c) Plutarch, *Table-Talk,* VIII 1, 2-3 (Loeb, *Moralia* 9, 114-19), has Apollo engender Plato not by seed, but by power; but the sequence seems to imply a form of intercourse, for it leads into the motif mentioned above regarding Egyptian belief. (d) The cult of Dusares at Petra and Hebron (and sometimes associated with Bethlehem) which is related to the mystery-cult acclamation of the virgin-mother goddess who has brought forth a son. See T. K. Cheyne, *Basic Problems and the New Material for Their Solution* (New York: Putnam, 1904), pp. 74-75. W. K. L. Clarke, *New Testament Problems* (London: Macmillan, 1929), pp. 1-5. This is another form of the Oriental fertility cult (Tammuz/Ishtar; Osiris/Isis), and the real parallels are to the Christian liturgical development of the Magi story into an epiphany celebration. No truly virginal conception is involved.

[105] I assume the common scholarly agreement that the Hebrew of Isa 7:14 has nothing to do with virginal conception. See pp. 15-16 above. D. Flusser, "The Son of Man," in *The Crucible of Christianity,* ed. A. Toynbee (London: Thames and Hudson, 1969), p. 229, calls attention to *Slavonic Enoch* and its statement that the mother of Melchizedek conceived her child through or from the Word of God. While this claim is interesting in the light of Qumran (and therefore pre-Christian) speculation about Melchizedek as a heavenly figure, *Slavonic Enoch* was written in the Christian period and so does not offer any real proof of a purely Jewish thesis of a virginal conception.

[106] See O. Michel and O. Betz, "Vom Gott gezeugt," *Judentum Urchristentum und Kirche,* ed. W. Eltester (J. Jeremias Festschrift; Berlin: Töpelmann, 1960), pp. 3-23. The banquet scene in 1QSa 2:11, at which the Messiah might appear, is scarcely the occasion for a virgin to conceive and bring forth a messianic child.

search because Matthew makes reference to the Greek (LXX) text of Isa 7:14, "The *virgin* shall conceive."[107] But we have no evidence that in Alexandrian Judaism the LXX of Isa 7:14 was understood to predict a virginal conception, since it need mean no more than that the girl who is now a virgin will ultimately conceive (in a natural way). Moreover, it is dubious that Isa 7:14 was the *origin* of Matthew's tradition of a virginal conception; elsewhere, including chapter 2, it is Matthew's custom to add fulfillment or formula citations to existing traditions.[108] And, indeed, there is no proof that Isa 7:14 played any major role in shaping the Lucan account of the virginal conception.

A parallel is sometimes sought in Philo's description of how virtues are generated in the human soul.[109] He employs allegorically the stories of the births of the patriarchs who were begotten through the instrumentality of God: "Rebekah, who is perseverance, became pregnant from God." Wary of seeking reliable parallelism in such an allegory, some have suggested that, underlying the Philonic exegesis, was a Hellenistic Jewish theory that the real patriarchs were conceived directly by God without male intervention. Paul has been thought to give witness to this in his distinction between Abraham's two sons, one born according to the flesh, one born according to the promise or spirit (Gal 4:23, 29).[110] Yet Rom 9:8-10 makes it clear that, for Paul, the patriarchal children of the promise were still conceived by

---

[107] See also the LXX rendering of Ps 110(109):3, "From the womb before the morning I have begotten you." Some think the LXX translators may have been influenced by the Egyptian ideas of royal birth (n. 103 above).

[108] K. Stendahl, *The School of St. Matthew* (rev. ed.; Philadelphia: Fortress, 1968), pp. vii-viii; W. Rothfuchs, *Die Erfüllungszitate des Matthäus-Evangeliums* (*BWANT* 88; Stuttgart: Kohlhammer, 1969), pp. 99-100.

[109] Philo, *De cherubim,* 12-15; but see also the other texts amassed by A. S. Carman, *American Journal of Theology* 9 (1905), 491-518. For the complexities of the symbolism see R. A. Baer, *Philo's Use of the Categories Male and Female* (Leiden: Brill, 1970). A careful discussion of the relevance of the Philonic material for the virginal conception is offered by Grelot (n. 29 above).

[110] R. H. Fuller, *Journal of Religion* 43 (1963), 254.

intercourse between their parents. And even if there were such a Hellenistic Jewish theory (and this remains possible), one still has to explain how it became embedded in some of the most Semitic sections of the NT.[111] Many scholars have proposed that the Lucan infancy narrative, especially chapter 1, was translated from Hebrew into Greek.[112] And Matthew's story of virginal conception is set in a background of peculiarly Galilean marriage customs.[113] And so no search for parallels has given us a truly satisfactory explanation of how early Christians happened upon the idea of a virginal conception[114]—unless, of course, that is what really took place.

(2) The charge of illegitimacy. Matthew tells us of the rumor that Mary's pregnancy was adulterous. The explanation given by the angel may have set Joseph's mind at ease; but in the implicit logic of Matthew's account there would have been no way to disguise the fact that Jesus would be born indecently

---

[111] W. D. Davies, *The Setting of the Sermon on the Mount* (Cambridge University, 1964), p. 64, recognizes the problem caused by the "extreme Jewishness" of the Matthean context; but when he seeks the parallel for the virginal conception in D. Daube's "trace of a Jewish legend of a conception without a human father, and the child in question may well be Moses," he has really moved into the realm of surmise (see pp. 81-82). The surmise may be correct, but the proof is inadequate.

[112] The debate raised by P. Winter is conveniently summarized by R. M. Wilson, *Studia Evangelica* I (*TU* 73; Berlin: Akademie, 1959) 235-53. The Semitic background of Luke 1:31-35 will be enhanced when J. T. Milik finally publishes an Aramaic fragment from Qumran (in possession since 1958) which contains this sentence: "He will be said to be son of God, and they will call him son of the Most High."

[113] The feeling against sexual relationship between betrothed (= married) who had not yet begun to live in the same house was stronger in Galilee than in Judea: Mishnah *Kethuboth* 1, 5; Babylonian Talmud *Kethuboth* 9b, 12a.

[114] Another field of exploration now opening is the Coptic Gnostic material from Nag Hammadi. Seemingly of Jewish origin, *The Apocalypse of Adam* (*CG* V, 78, 18-20) refers, apparently in a hostile manner, to the third kingdom of him who came from a virgin womb.

early after Mary was taken to Joseph's home. Obviously Matthew is facing a story that is in circulation and factual data that he cannot deny: he does not and seemingly cannot reply that Jesus was born at the proper interval after Joseph and Mary came to live together. Traces of the rumor of irregularity of birth and illegitimacy appear elsewhere in the NT. The reference to Jesus as "son of Mary" (Mark 6:3) is strange, for generally sons were not called by their mother's name unless paternity was uncertain or unknown.[115] Illegitimacy may be implied in the retort of "the Jews" in John 8:41, *"We* were not born illegitimate," if the Greek *hēmeis* is emphatic by way of contrast. And certainly, from the time of Origen through the Talmud and the medieval legends of the *Toledoth Yeshu,* the constant Jewish refutation of Christian claims about Jesus' origins has not been that he was an ordinary child, the legitimate son of Joseph, but that his mother committed adultery with another and he was born illegitimate.[116] Since it is not easy to dismiss such a persistent charge, which may be as old as Christianity itself, those who deny the virginal conception cannot escape the task of explaining how the rumor of illegitimacy and irregularity of birth arose and how they would answer it without accepting a very unpleasant alternative.

*   *   *

My judgment, in conclusion, is that the totality of the *scientifically controllable* evidence leaves an unresolved problem[117]

[115] E. Stauffer, "Jeschu ben Mirjam," *Neotestamentica et Semitica,* ed. E. E. Ellis and M. Wilcox, in honour of M. Black (Edinburgh: Clark, 1969), pp. 119-28.

[116] The Samaritan Chronicle of A.D. 1616, just published by J. Macdonald and A. J. B. Higgins, *New Testament Studies* 19 (1971-72), 54-80, constitutes an exception since it reports the Jewish adversaries as saying that Jesus was the son of Joseph—but still his *illegitimate* son because he lay with Mary before the proper time. The value of the evidence is dubious because there is clear dependence on Matthew's Gospel.

[117] In particular, as a Roman Catholic whose biblical studies have led him to appreciate all the more the importance of a teaching

—a conclusion that should not disappoint since I used the word "problem" in my title—and that is why I want to induce an honest, ecumenical discussion of it. Part of the difficulty is that past discussions have often been conducted by people who were interpreting ambiguous evidence to favor positions already taken.

I would urge, however, that this discussion be pursued in an atmosphere of pastoral responsibility. I have already warned that here we are touching on the ordinary Protestant and the ordinary Catholic principles of authority, namely, Bible and Church teaching, and so even an openness to discussion will confuse and frighten many. Moreover, there is the danger that the discussion might imperil a traditional formulation of faith that has served Christianity well, and those who discuss the matter must show a sensitivity for the underlying beliefs that have been formulated in terms of virginal conception.[118] For instance, the idea that through the power of the Holy Spirit Jesus was conceived of Mary a virgin has helped to emphasize both the reality of Jesus' humanity and his uniqueness as God's Son. The virginal conception also has given *a woman* a central role in Christianity, and today we should appreciate more than ever before what a service that was. Leaving aside Protestant minimalism and Catholic exaggeration in Mariology, can any of us fail to see that, in all those centuries when no woman could stand publicly in the sanctuaries of churches, it was symbolically significant that a statue of the Virgin stood there. If by Church law a woman could not preside at the ceremonies that brought about Jesus' eucharistic presence, no one could deny that by God's law it was a woman and not a man who

---

Church, I cannot resolve the problem independently of the question of authority raised in Section II. I am not afraid that an honest discussion of the virginal conception will lead to a traumatic choice between fidelity to modern exegesis and fidelity to a teaching Church, provided that both the Bible and tradition are subjected to intelligent historical criticism to find out exactly what was meant and the degree to which it was affirmed. Inevitably, however, openness to discussion will be misrepresented as denial of tradition.

[118] See n. 57 above.

brought about Jesus' historical presence. It must be with an awareness of what the virginal conception has meant to Christianity that we theologians and church historians and exegetes begin our ecumenical discussion of it. Discuss it we must, for Christianity can never seek refuge in anything except the truth, painful as it may be. But as we discuss Mary's virginity, we must assure all those ordinary people in our churches, the "little people" who happen to be God's people, that in our quest we "experts" have not forgotten that we too must obey the biblical injunction (Luke 1:48) that all generations, even this "nosey" generation, shall call her blessed.

CHAPTER TWO
THE PROBLEM OF THE
BODILY RESURRECTION
OF JESUS[119]

"If Christ has not been raised, then our preaching is in vain, and your faith is in vain" (I Cor 15:14). "I believe in Jesus Christ, His only Son, our Lord, . . . the third day he rose again from the dead" (Apostles' Creed). Jesus' victory over death has been a fundamental Christian concern from the beginning until the present day.[120] Since the NT and the Apostles' Creed

---

[119] This chapter has not been published before. For previous reflections see my articles, "The Resurrection and Biblical Criticism," *Commonweal* (Nov. 24, 1967), pp. 232-36; and "The Resurrection of Jesus," art. 76, §§146-59, in *The Jerome Biblical Commentary* (n. 2 above).

[120] The bibliography is vast; here I give preference to works in English to help the type of reader for whom this book is intended. The following works are basic (in citing them only the authors' names will be used): Benoit, P., *The Passion and Resurrection of Jesus Christ* (New York: Herder and Herder, 1969); Evans, C. F., *Resurrection and the New Testament* (Studies in Biblical Theology, II #12; London: SCM, 1970); Fuller, R. H., *The Formation of the Resurrection Narratives* (New York: Macmillan, 1971); Léon-Dufour, X., *Résurrection de Jésus et message pascal* (Paris: Seuil, 1971); Marxsen, W., *The Resurrection of Jesus of Nazareth* (Philadelphia: Fortress, 1970).

Marxsen will be cited frequently because his views have catalyzed discussion, but note the careful review of his book by G. O'Collins, *The Heythrop Journal* 12 (1971), 207-11: "Marxsen's exegesis in-speak insistently of that victory in terms of Jesus being raised or risen, it is difficult *prima facie* to understand why some theologians today, both Catholic and Protestant, are asking whether resurrection language should be preserved. On the one hand, they wonder whether it is meaningful to modern man; on the other, they question whether the concept of resurrection from the grave (because that is certainly what resurrection meant to the Jews of Jesus' time)[121] is sufficiently accurate to describe what happened. As with the problem of the virginal conception, the problem of whether Jesus was raised bodily from the dead may seem to some the depth of irrelevancy, since it is the type of historical question that will scarcely change the life of modern man or even the life of the modern Christian. I can only repeat my answer that questions which deal with the uniqueness of Jesus—with the moments of God's eschatological intervention on behalf of Jesus, and surely the resurrection is one, along with the incarnation—can never become irrelevant to Christians, except at the price of making Christianity itself irrelevant.

I. The State of the Problem

When I say that theologians are questioning the validity of resurrection language, I do not necessarily mean that they are questioning the importance of Jesus' victory over death, which

---

spires less and less confidence as it gradually becomes more obvious that dogmatic convictions are in control." While I disagree in some important points with Léon-Dufour (whose work is based on a more trenchant biblical criticism than is used by Benoit, the other Catholic in the above list), I wish to dissociate myself vigorously from the vicious criticism, stemming from Catholic reactionaries, that has greeted the publishing of his book in Europe. I wish there was as comprehensive a work by a Catholic in English. Fuller and Evans offer the most useful compendia in the list, with Fuller having the edge for classroom utility.

[121] It is not really accurate to claim that the NT references to the *resurrection* of Jesus are ambiguous as to whether they mean bodily resurrection—there was no other kind of resurrection. Ambiguity arises only about the kind of body involved (earthly, celestial, etc.).

is the Christian mystery that underlies resurrection language. In Roman Catholic theology in particular, Jesus' victory over death, too long seen primarily as an apologetic proof, has moved into the limelight of theological and spiritual reflection.[122] In the debates that surrounded the Second Vatican Council, it was considered a victory of the modern theological movement to have redemption through Christ described as effected not only by his death but also by his resurrection from the dead. Yet, despite the renewed importance of resurrection theology, the problem of the aptness of resurrection language to describe the victory is very much with us.

Once again, as we saw in proposing to discuss the virginal conception of Jesus, the thought of questioning an ancient formulation produces strong reactions. Liberals, for whom fidelity to the NT is not a major issue,[123] will instinctively feel sympathetic toward the possibility of divesting Christianity of something so antiquated as the imagery of a dead body coming to life. And fundamentalists, who are incapable of distinguishing between a truth and its formulation,[124] will immediately conclude that a questioning of resurrection language represents a loss of faith in Jesus' triumph over death.

Catholics involved in modern biblical studies cannot afford

---

[122] Still a classic in this vein is F. X. Durrwell, *The Resurrection: A Biblical Study* (New York: Sheed and Ward, 1960); see also D. M. Stanley, *Christ's Resurrection in Pauline Soteriology* (Analecta Biblica 13; Rome: Pontifical Biblical Institute, 1961). While I regard the problem of the bodily resurrection important enough to warrant a chapter of this small book, I hope that my readers understand that such a discussion is only a prolegomenon to the more positive contributions that modern biblical research has made concerning the resurrection.

[123] The existence of this type of liberalism in modern Roman Catholicism merits attention. The conservative Catholic theological thought of the last centuries has been dominated by a medieval philosophical system and has not been primarily based on the Scriptures. The shift to the left and to a liberal theology has too often meant only that a new, modern philosophy, equally unbiblical, has been substituted for an older one.

[124] See the discussion of this point above in the Introduction, pp. 7-15.

the luxury of such doctrinaire attitudes. It has become apparent to us, as it did to our Protestant confreres earlier, that the language or imagery of the NT is not always so essentially related to what it describes that it cannot be substituted for without detriment to the reality. (Indeed, often when it cannot be substituted for, it may still need to be qualified.) Frequently the relation of NT language and imagery to truth is pedagogic but not essential, and modern theology may have to complement the NT by discovering another language or imagery to speak to the men of our times. Thus, each theological problem has to be examined in the light of contemporary biblical criticism to find, to the best of our ability, the real intent of the language of the NT and to see whether that intent is still conveyed by repeating the ancient formulas. The fact that creedal terminology involving bodily resurrection has been found satisfactory for a long time should make us very cautious about change, but even long usage does not render terminology irreplaceable. On the other hand, if a critical modern investigation shows that as far back as we can trace in the NT evidence, resurrection from the dead was an intrinsic part of Jesus' victory over death, then the observation that modern man does not find bodily resurrection appealing or meaningful cannot be determinative. Nor, as we saw with the virginal conception, can we allow Christian theology to be shaped by the contemporary distrust of the miraculous. The modern world view is no more infallible than the first-century world view—it knows more about some things but is less perceptive in other ways. Our generation must be obedient, as were our predecessors, to what *God* has chosen to do in Jesus; and we cannot impose on the picture what we think God should have done.

Laying aside these fundamentalist and liberal prejudices, let us move on to at least three different attitudes that believing theologians (and I emphasize "believing") have manifested in questioning the applicability of the language of bodily resurrection. *First,* some who would never admit that Jesus' body corrupted to dust in the tomb feel, nevertheless, that resurrection language, as popularly understood, undervalues the transformation that took place in the victory over death granted by God to Jesus. It is probably true that a great number of Christians who believe in the resurrection of Jesus have confused this resurrection with the resuscitation of a corpse. For instance, many see no difference between the risen Jesus and the people whom Jesus is reported to have restored to ordinary life during his ministry (Lazarus, the daughter of Jairus, the son of the widow of Nain). This is a confusion because the NT evidence is lucidly clear that Jesus was *not* restored to ordinary life—his risen existence is glorious and eschatological, transported beyond the limitations of space and time; and he will not die again. Yet, while one must sympathize with the desire of theologians to remove the causes of such confusion about the risen state of Jesus, one may well wonder if an abandonment of resurrection language is not too drastic a remedy. Perhaps we could insist on using "resuscitation" to describe the Gospel miracles by which Jesus restored men to natural life and on keeping "resurrection" to describe the unique eschatological event by which Jesus was elevated from the tomb to glory.

Second, there are believing theologians whose difficulty about resurrection language is more than terminological, for they are not certain that Jesus' body did not corrupt in the grave. Perhaps we could call them agnostic about the fate of Jesus' body. "Resurrection" is a possible way of describing Jesus' victory, but for them there are other ways which are even more fitting in that they preserve an ambiguity about the "how" of that victory. It is pointed out that at times the NT itself uses non-resurrectional imagery to describe Jesus' victory over death. Let us pause to examine some of the proposed alternatives, for they are not without difficulty:

(a) In Hebrews 9:11-12 Jesus is pictured as a high priest entering "through the greater and more perfect tabernacle, not made with hands," into the heavenly Holy Place with his own blood that was shed in sacrifice (also 4:14; 6:19-20). The language is symbolic and obscure but some have read it to imply a direct progression from crucifixion to ascension without an intervening act of resurrection. However, others have argued that the "greater and more perfect tabernacle" is a reference

to the risen body of Jesus.[125] What is certain is that the author
of Hebrews did not reject the idea of resurrection from the dead,
because in 13:20 he speaks of God's having "brought again
from the dead our Lord Jesus" (cf. also 11:19).

(b) Another alternative to resurrection language in the NT
is sought in the "exaltation" language of liturgical and hymnic
passages: "God has highly exalted him" (Philip 2:9); "He
ascended high above all the heavens" (Eph 4:10); "He was
taken up into glory" (I Tim 3:16). It is quite clear, of course,
that the authors who speak of Jesus' exaltation into glory do
not disbelieve in his resurrection from the dead, for the same
Paul who wrote Philippians wrote I Cor 15:3-8.[126] Yet scholars
suggest that two ways of describing Jesus' victory, once quite
different, have been harmonized by NT authors, and that originally exaltation into heaven did not imply resurrection from the
dead. It is very difficult to be certain of this claim, for "exaltation" need have done no more than capture the eschatological
aspect of the resurrection.[127]

(c) Still another alternative to resurrection language is supposedly found in the NT affirmation that *Jesus lives,* e.g., "He
was crucified in weakness but lives by the power of God" (II
Cor 13:4; also Rom 14:9). However, a close comparison of
this affirmation with other NT formulas that speak of resurrection suggests that "lives" is just another way of saying "was
raised." For instance, we may set the citation just made from

---

[125] For the literature see M. Bourke, *The Jerome Biblical Commentary* (n. 2 above), art. 61, §51. Marxsen, p. 145, is not convincing in his argument that, while the author of Hebrews uses the
language of resurrection, he means no more than exaltation. This
is bending the evidence to fit a theory.

[126] Notice the combination of the exaltation motif ("ascend")
with the resurrection in Rom 10:6-7.

[127] There is a discussion of different views on the relation of resurrection and exaltation in Evans, pp. 135-43, and Léon-Dufour, pp.
55-75. The latter argues that, although exaltation language appears
in the Christian hymns of the NT, it is not necessarily later than
resurrection language which appears in the primitive kerygma or
proclamation. Yet he recognizes that one cannot claim that resurrection language is derivative from exaltation language.

II Corinthians alongside the formula in Acts 2:23-24: "You crucified this Jesus . . . but God raised him up." See also Luke 24:23 where the affirmation that Jesus was alive is associated with the discovery of the empty tomb. Thus, for the NT, the perduring life of Jesus is the end result of his having been raised from the dead, not an alternative to his resurrection.[128]

And so it is not really clear that any of the "alternative" language for Jesus' victory over death existed in Christianity independently of a belief in Jesus' resurrection from the dead. Similarly there is difficulty with the process of the development of resurrection language that is sometimes proposed by those who are agnostic about the fate of Jesus' body. It is suggested that somehow a genuine faith in Jesus' victory over death emerged and that this faith was conceptualized as bodily resurrection, not on a factual basis (whether by encounter with the risen Jesus or by interpretation of the empty tomb) but simply

---

[128] On the lips of some modern theologians, however, "Jesus lives" is meant as a real alternative to "Jesus was raised" or "Jesus is risen," a formula which they find unsatisfactory. I asked a prominent Catholic proponent of the affirmation "Jesus lives" how he understood this to differ from a similar affirmation that could be made about the saintly dead: "Francis of Assisi lives; Karl Barth lives." I was told that the difference consisted in the fact that Jesus *started* this process of new life and was the first born of the dead. However, if I understand correctly, the NT authors are saying that God has done an eschatological act in Jesus that He has not yet done for Jesus' followers, living or dead—God *has* raised Jesus; He *will* raise Jesus' followers. Another modern non-resurrectional formula for describing Jesus' victory is Marxsen's "The activity of Jesus goes on" (p. 77); "The cause of Jesus continues" (p. 141). However, it is not totally clear to what extent Marxsen believes that the person of Jesus survives as distinct from his cause, especially when he says, "Jesus is dead. But *his* offer has not thereby lost its validity" (p. 147).

In general, theologians can speculate about the many ways God could have made Jesus victorious, but the NT gives the only real evidence about what God actually did. If that evidence, critically studied, allows several possible theological analyses, fine. But a theological stance that does not do justice to the biblical evidence is of little value, no matter how possible or attractive it may be in itself.

because *the Jewish mind had available no other concept for expressing a victory over death.* This contention is inaccurate, for we know of several other models of victory over death that were current in Judaism and might have been employed by Christians, models that did not involve the resurrection and/or appearances of the one raised from the dead. For instance, the Gospels draw parallels between Jesus and Elijah; and so it would not have been unusual for Christians to have preached that, like Elijah, Jesus was assumed into heaven and that he would return at the last judgment. In the Book of Wisdom the survival after death of the just who had been persecuted is described in terms of an immortality (of a soul-like principle) granted by God: "The souls of the just are in the hand of God, and no torment shall touch them. They seemed in the view of the foolish to be dead, and their passing away was thought to be an affliction . . . but they shall be greatly blessed, because God tried them and found them worthy of Himself. As sacrificial offerings, he took them to himself . . . they shall judge nations and rule over peoples" (Wisdom 3:1-8). Since this concept of immortality was scarcely confined to the Greek-speaking Jews of Alexandria who composed the Book of Wisdom, Jesus' fate could have been described in a similar manner without any more resort to resurrection than is found in Wisdom. Thus the choice of resurrection language was not an inevitability for the early Jews who believed in Jesus. To the contrary, its choice must be explained; for, while there was an expectation among many Jews of the resurrection of the dead in the last times, there was no expectation of the resurrection of a single man from the dead, separate from and preliminary to the general resurrection.[129]

Third, a final group of believing theologians are yet more radical in their displeasure with resurrection language. They do not seek possible alternatives of equal value, for they regard resurrection language as falsification. They are not agnostic

---

[129] The tendency to unite Jesus' resurrection with the general resurrection is exemplified in Matt 27:53 where we are told that after Jesus' resurrection many of the saints came out of their tombs and went into the holy city of Jerusalem and appeared to many.

about the bodily resurrection, since they think it clear that Jesus' body did decompose in Palestine. For them, the emergence of his body from the tomb was a primitive and mythological way of describing a victory that totally defied human description and experience. In confronting these theologians, it is useless for more conservative Christians to repeat the quotation from Paul given at the beginning of this chapter—they would agree with Paul on the truth and importance of Jesus' victory over death, but they do not agree with his way of describing that victory.

In order to deal with this variety of opinions about the unsuitability of resurrection language we must examine as objectively as possible (according to the methods of biblical criticism[130]) the NT material pertinent to the bodily resurrection of Jesus. Unlike the concept of a virginal conception for which, as we saw, there is very limited attestation in the NT, the theme that Jesus has been raised from the dead is found in all four Gospels, in Acts, in most of the epistolary literature, and in the Apocalypse (Revelation). Indeed, the affirmative evidence for a bodily resurrection is so widespread that our quest may seem foolish to the ordinary student of the Bible. Yet, when one reflects that the oldest extant NT book (I Thessalonians) dates from about A.D. 50, a date twenty years after the resurrection events, one realizes that the quantity of evidence does not necessarily solve our problem about the *original* understanding of Jesus' victory over death. In treating the evidence we shall seek to follow the pattern of chronological development, beginning with early formulations found in the Pauline letters and in the sermons narrated in the Book of Acts,[131] and then moving on to the narratives of Jesus' appearances and of

---

[130] See n. 9 above.

[131] The generally accepted thesis today is that the Book of Acts was composed in the 80's or 90's, and that its references to Christian origins sometimes reflect the Lucan theology of the late first century rather than a historical memory of the situation in the 30's and 40's. Nevertheless, in the sermons that Luke attributes to Peter and Paul (scarcely verbatim reports but examples of an early style of kerygmatic proclamation), he preserves ancient expressions from the Church's beginnings.

the finding of the empty tomb (narratives preserved in Gospels which were written after the Pauline letters).

II. The Earliest Christian Formulations of Resurrection Faith

Our earliest material consists of short formulas about the risen[132] Jesus that were current in the preaching, the catechesis, the liturgy, and the confessions of faith of the early Christians. As Fuller, p. 16, sagely remarks, "In the early community, the resurrection was not narrated but proclaimed." These formulas vary in style and length and are often classified according to whether they have one, two, or four clauses (members). For our purposes, we can treat together the shorter formulas and then concentrate on the famous Pauline formula in I Cor 15.

(A) The Shorter Formulas

The one-member NT formula mentions only the resurrection of Jesus, and not the preliminaries of crucifixion, death, and burial. Sometimes the divine agency is specified: God raised Jesus from the dead.[133] Other times as in Luke 24:34, the agency of God is implied through the divine passive: "The Lord was raised indeed!"

While such a formula is not particularly helpful in our quest

---

[132] Two Greek verbs (with related nouns) are employed in the resurrection language of the NT: *egeirein* and *anistanai*. The former was scarcely ever used in secular Greek for resurrection of the dead but covered a broad range of ideas of raising, lifting, and awakening. The latter had some application in Hellenistic Greek for the raising of the dead. It is difficult to be certain of the primary imagery involved in these verbs, e.g., to awaken the dead from sleep; to make the dead stand upright; to draw the deceased out of or up from the abode of the dead, etc. Probably the root meaning of the verbs contributed little to the Christian theology of resurrection. See Evans, pp. 20-26.

[133] I Thess 1:10; I Cor 6:14; Gal 1:1; Rom 4:24; 8:11; 10:9; Acts 17:31.

about the bodily resurrection, perhaps this is the best time to explain once for all what is involved in the passive expression "was raised," since many Christians seem to find it threateningly ambiguous about Jesus' divine status. In some twenty passages the NT makes it clear that God the Father (subject) raised Jesus (object) from the dead. The earliest Christian tradition attributed the agency in the resurrection to the heavenly Father. In a number of passages, especially in the Gospels (Mark 16:6; Matt 28:6, 7; Luke 24:6, 34) Jesus is the subject of the verbal form *egerthē,* an aorist passive form of *egeirein,* normally to be translated "was raised." Another translation ("is risen") is possible because in the Koine Greek of the NT world such passive forms could be meant intransitively with an active nuance. When Jerome translated the Greek NT into Latin, he chose the "is risen" translation and used the active Latin form *surrexit* to render *egerthē.* Since, up to the Second Vatican Council, all official English Catholic New Testaments were translated from Jerome's Latin, Catholics were familiar only with the "is risen" translation. When the New American Bible translation was made by Catholic scholars from the Greek, they made the wise choice of generally preferring "Jesus was raised" (by God) as a translation in harmony with the explicit early Christian references to God's activity in the resurrection, as mentioned above.[134] By the A.D. 90's, if not before, christology had developed to such a point that the Fourth Evangelist could state that Jesus and the Father act by the same divine power (John 10:30) and that therefore it could be said that Jesus

---

[134] Some Catholic fundamentalists immediately detected a plot upon the part of the translators to deny the divinity of Jesus. Triumphantly they posed what they thought was the unanswerable question: if Jesus did not rise but was raised, who raised him? Such a reaction betrays the very limited extent to which modern historical approaches have filtered down through Catholicism even though they have been officially approved by Pope and Council. What is said above about the early Christian understanding of the resurrection is intelligible only if we accept the fact that the Christian appreciation of the way God was present in Christ Jesus (II Cor 5:19) was a slow process spanning the NT and beyond (and still not finished!).

rose by his own power (10:17-18).[135] This trend becomes even more explicit in second-century Christian writings: "He truly raised himself" (Ignatius, *Smyrnaeans* 2:1); "He transformed (himself) into an imperishable eon and raised himself up" (*Epistle to Rheginos* 45:17ff.).

The shortest formula about Jesus' resurrection obviously interpreted that event against the background of the Jewish expectation of what God was to do for the just in the last days. The Christian formula echoes the first-century A.D. Jewish prayer found in the second of the "Eighteen Benedictions" (*Shemoneh Esreh*): "You are mighty forever, O Lord, humbling the proud, judging the powerful, living through the centuries, *raising the dead*, ... Blessed are you, O Lord, who give life to the dead."[136] But the Christian understanding of what God had done was vividly colored by the kind of death Jesus had died, and this understanding found expression in two-member formulas. Sometimes the mention of the death is without evaluation as if death and resurrection were a simple sequence: "Jesus died and rose [*anistanai*]" (I Thess 4:14); "Christ died and lived again" (Rom 14:9). More often the death is seen as a clear antithesis to the resurrection: "You crucified this Jesus ... but God raised him up" (Acts 2:23-24; 4:10; 5:30-31; 10:39-40). While the anti-Jewish element in these formulas of Acts may be a later development (as also the redemptive note in Rom 4:25: "Put to death *for our trespasses* and raised *for our justification*"), the antithesis between death and resurrection is probably more original than the smooth sequence, for in the Jewish milieu the crucifixion was a scandal and not simply a preliminary to the resurrection.[137]

---

[135] I assume here the common position of Johannine scholars, Catholic and Protestant, that the statements attributed to Jesus in John often reflect the theology of the evangelist at the end of the century rather than an exact historical memory of the words of Jesus during his ministry. See n. 14 and n. 64 above.

[136] The Palestinian text (as distinct from the more developed Babylonian text) is given by G. Dalman, *Die Worte Jesu* (Leipzig: Hinrich, 1898), p. 299.

[137] The contrast between what man did (namely, crucified Jesus)

(B) The Formula in I Corinthians 15:3-8

The more developed formula of four members that Paul cites in his Corinthian correspondence[138] is of major import. Not only is it the only NT testimony to the resurrection written by one who claims to have seen the risen Jesus, but also it is one of the most ancient NT references to the events that surrounded the resurrection. Although Paul wrote I Corinthians about the year A.D. 56, he tells the Corinthians (15:3) that what he *transmitted* to them (presumably when he first came to Corinth about 50) was information that he himself had *received* at an earlier period. The verbs "transmit" and "receive" are almost technical terms in the vocabulary of Judaism for the handing on of tradition,[139] so that we are dealing here, at least in part, with a primitive tradition from Paul's early days as a Christian (mid-30's?).[140]

---

and what God did by reaction (raised Jesus up) is called a re-active understanding of the resurrection. As Evans, p. 133, points out, it is a rudimentary understanding giving little positive value to the cross. Its presence in Acts indicates pre-Lucan thought.

[138] A complete treatment is offered by J. Kremer, *Das älteste Zeugnis von der Auferstehung Christi* (Stuttgarter Bibelstudien 17; Katholisches Bibelwerk, 1966). For a convenient English survey see F. Foulkes, "Some Aspects of St. Paul's Treatment of the Resurrection of Christ in I Corinthians XV," *Australasian Biblical Review* 16 (1968), 15-30.

[139] See the article on *paradidōmi* ("receive") by F. Büchsel and on *paralambanō* ("transmit") by G. Delling in *Theological Dictionary of the New Testament*, ed. G. Kittel, II, 171-73, and IV, 12-14.

[140] J. Jeremias, *The Eucharistic Words of Jesus* (New York: Scribner's, 1966), pp. 101-3, has argued that the original language of this formula was Aramaic, raising the possibility that it stems from the earliest Palestinian stratum of Christianity. H. Conzelmann, "On the Analysis of the Confessional Formula in I Cor. 15. 3-5," *Interpretation* 20 (1966), 15-25, rejects Jeremias' theory and argues for a non-Pauline Greek original, and thus posits that the formula originated after Christianity had spread to Greek-speaking communities. Fuller, p. 11, suggests that at least the content of the formula is Palestinian, even if the formula, as Paul cites it, has been

I Corinthians 15:3-8

³For I transmitted to you as of first importance what I also received:
    that Christ died for our sins according to the Scriptures;
⁴and *that* he was buried;
 and *that* he was raised on the third day according to the Scriptures;
⁵and *that* he appeared:
        [1] to Cephas,
        [2] then to the Twelve;
⁶[3] and then he appeared to more than 500 brethren at one
            time, of whom most remain alive until now, though some
            have fallen asleep.
⁷And then he appeared:
        [4] to James,
        [5] then to all the apostles;
⁸[6] last of all, as to one irregularly born, he appeared also to
            me.

Obviously only part of the Corinthian passage can constitute
what Paul "received" as primitive Christian tradition; for example, a reference to the appearance of Jesus to Paul himself
(the sixth appearance listed) cannot have been part of that
tradition. Where then did the original, pre-Pauline formula stop?
One view is that it stopped with "he appeared" and thus without
listing the recipients of the appearances. This would mean that
the "transmitted" tradition consisted of four "that" (*hoti*)
clauses: "that Christ died . . . and that he was buried; and that
he was raised . . . and that he appeared." These four clauses
would have a balance because the first and the third were length-
ened by qualifying phrases, respectively: "*died* for our sins
according to the Scriptures"; "*raised* on the third day according
to the Scriptures." Moreover, the (appended) list of six appearances would also have a balance, for there are two groups
of three appearances. Within these two groups, appearance [1]
matches appearance [4] in length and in subject (one person);

Hellenized. On p. 14 Fuller specifies that the first part of the
formula (vss. 3-4) may have come from the Damascus region
where Paul was converted, whereas the information in the last part
(vss. 5-8), dealing with the appearances, may have come from
Jerusalem (or Palestine).

similarly appearance [2] matches appearance [5]; and appearance [3] matches appearance [6], at least in length. We shall adopt this analysis as a working hypothesis, cautioning, however, that other analyses of what constituted the pre-Pauline formula are possible.[141]

(1) *The sequence of death, burial, resurrection, and appearance(s).* We see that the four "that" clauses of the pre-Pauline formula concern, not just death and resurrection, as in the two-member formulas, but a whole chain of events. Thus we have the skeleton of what will emerge in the Gospels as a consecutive narrative. Moreover, the notion of the fulfillment of Scripture is woven into clauses one and three; and it was precisely the Church's quest for OT background that fleshed out the death and post-resurrection narratives of the Gospels, where fulfillment of Scripture is a major theme. (For instance, note how strongly this motif has been introduced in Luke 24:25-27.)

Some would find in the pre-Pauline formula, at least by implication, the first recorded reference to the empty tomb in Jerusalem. Yet to read a hint of the empty tomb in the refer-

---

[141] In particular, some have thought it unlikely that the pre-Pauline formula could have ended with the bald statement "he appeared" without some designation of the recipient(s) of the appearance(s). One suggestion is that the pre-Pauline formula included Cephas on the analogy of Luke 24:34: "The Lord has been raised and has appeared to Simon." (This proposal often carries with it the innuendo that the appearance to Cephas was the oldest and most reliable tradition and that all Christian faith was a development from it—see Marxsen, pp. 88ff.) Another suggestion would include appearances to both Cephas and the Twelve in the formula, because an appearance to the Twelve seems to stand at the very foundation of the Church and of the early missionary efforts and so could scarcely have been neglected. On the other hand, some doubt that there was even a unit of four "that" clauses in the pre-Pauline formula. Fuller, pp. 13-14, prefers U. Wilckens' analysis that it was Paul who combined four different formulas, each introduced by *hoti*, which serves the function of a new set of quotation marks. It is too demanding on coincidence, however, that four independent formulas would have resulted in the careful balance of alternating length now found in the "that" clauses of I Cor 15:3-5.

ence to Jesus' burial goes beyond the evidence,[142] for the formula's sequence of death, burial, resurrection, and appearance is meant primarily to bring out an element of continuity. The Jesus who died and was buried is the same Jesus who was raised and appeared. This continuity, as we shall see, is an important element in the idea of bodily resurrection, but it tells us nothing about an empty tomb. Later (p. 124 below) we shall discuss whether the fact that Jesus' body was no longer in the tomb is implied in the affirmation "he was raised on the third day."

What is significant in this formula is that for the first time a reference is made to the appearance(s) of the risen Jesus.[143] While most scholars think that faith in Jesus' victory over death was first engendered by his appearance(s) to his followers, it is interesting that the shorter formulas considered above do not mention an appearance. Perhaps this is because they were formulated by those to whom the risen Jesus had appeared,

---

[142] Several questions must be distinguished. Paul may have known of the tradition of the empty tomb of Jesus in Jerusalem (according to Gal 1:18 Paul went to Jerusalem to confer with Cephas) without ever having referred to this tradition, even implicitly. Moreover, Paul may have proclaimed that Jesus was raised bodily from the tomb without ever knowing of a tradition that Jesus' tomb stood empty in Jerusalem. I find ample evidence for Paul's believing that Jesus' body had been raised from the tomb so that he has become the firstborn of the dead (Rom 8:29; I Cor 15:23). For instance, in Rom 6:4 Paul compares Christian baptism to being buried with Christ, "so that as Christ was raised from the dead by the glory of the Father, we too might walk in the newness of life" (also Col 2:12). But I think the evidence for an implicit Pauline reference to the finding of an empty tomb in Jerusalem is more speculative. (To the contrary see J. Mánek, "The Apostle Paul and the Empty Tomb," *Novum Testamentum* 2 [1957], 276-80.)

[143] In the theory that Fuller adopts (n. 141 above), not only the list of recipients of appearances but the very fact that Jesus appeared is Paul's addition to the original kerygmatic formulas in I Cor 15:3-4. However, we note Luke 24:34 where both "raised" and "appeared to Simon" are part of a pre-Lucan kerygmatic formula.

men whose very activity as proclaimers of the risen Lord testified implicitly to such an appearance.

What does this formula in I Corinthians with its reference to appearances tell us about the risen Jesus? In the later Gospel narratives the post-resurrectional appearances of Jesus are understood in a bodily, indeed even a physical, way. For instance, in Luke 24:39 the risen Jesus says, "See my hands and my feet, that it is I myself; handle me and see; for a spirit has not flesh and bones as you see that I have." Jesus then takes fish and eats it before them. The invitation to Thomas to probe the hands and side of the risen Jesus (John 20:27) and the reference to a meal in John 21:10-13 may have a similar implication of tangible reality. But are these chronologically late narratives necessarily in harmony with the earliest understanding of the appearances of Jesus, or are they apologetic developments[144] designed to refute the charge that the disciples did not really see Jesus but only an apparition?

How did Paul, who himself claims to have "seen" the risen Jesus, understand the nature of Jesus' appearance(s)? It seems that he thought Jesus had risen bodily from the dead but paradoxically he rejected the idea that the risen body was natural or physical.[145] The evidence for this is found in the rest of chapter 15 of I Corinthians which goes on to treat of the

---

[144] Surmises about apologetic developments involve using the sacred writer's comments as a mirror for detecting the charges made by his opponents. Thus, Luke's insistent rejection of the idea that the risen Jesus was a spirit is a good indication of what those hostile to the resurrection were saying. Similarly, from Acts 10:41 we may deduce that the opponents were objecting to why, if Jesus had really appeared, he was seen by only a few people.

[145] Many Christians today see only two possibilities: either one affirms a corporeal resurrection so physical that the risen Jesus was just as tangible as he was during his lifetime; or one denies the corporeal resurrection and reduces the appearances to an internal awareness of Jesus' spiritual victory. However, there is a middle ground, namely, a corporeal resurrection in which the risen body is transformed to the eschatological sphere, no longer bound by space and time—a body that no longer has all the natural or physical characteristics that marked its temporal existence.

resurrection of Christian believers, a resurrection patterned on the resurrection of Jesus.[146] In 15:35ff. Paul emphasizes the tremendous transformation that is involved in resurrection—the present or terrestial body is to the resurrected or celestial body as the kernel of grain sown in the ground is to the wheat that emerges from the ground. In vss. 42-44 Paul says, "So it is with the resurrection of the dead:

What is sown is perishable; what is raised is imperishable.
It is sown in dishonor; it is raised in glory.
It is sown in weakness; it is raised in power.
It is sown a physical [*psychikos*] body; it is raised a spiritual body."

Further on (vs. 50) he states, "Flesh and blood cannot inherit the kingdom of God." In these verses Paul seems to proclaim a *corporeal resurrection,* for he speaks insistently of body.[147]

---

[146] The thesis that the Pauline conceptions of the two resurrections are not connected (H. Grass) is rightly rejected by Fuller, pp. 20-21, in light of Philip 3:20-21: "The Lord Jesus Christ, who will change our lowly body to be like his glorious body" (also Rom 8:11).

[147] Paul's picture of the resurrected body in I Cor 15 is not without difficulty. When Paul says that the risen body is not *psychikos* (as opposed to *pneumatikos* or "spiritual"), what does he mean? The Revised Standard Version accepts the translation "physical"; the New American Bible has "natural"; the New English Bible has "animal." Clearly Paul rejects a crassly material conception whereby the risen body would resume the qualities of life as we know it —a conception that was current in Paul's time, as we see in II Baruch 50:2: "For the earth shall then assuredly restore the dead. . . . It shall make no change in their form; but as it has received them, so it shall restore them." Paul seems to posit a transformation and spiritualization of the earthly body. Other scholars, however, suggest that Paul is thinking not of a transformation but of an exchange: a spiritual body replacing the earthly body. (See T. E. Pollard, "The Body of the Resurrection," *Colloquium* 2 [1967], 105-15, esp. p. 109.) They cite II Cor 5:1: "If the earthly tent we live in is destroyed, we have a building from God, a house not made with hands, eternal in the heavens." Yet it should be noted that II Cor 5, which does not deal with the resurrection of Jesus at all, may have moved on to a new problem, namely, how the faithful dead live with Christ in the interim between death and

Of course, "body" did not mean for Paul what it means for most Christians today, since his basic anthropology did not involve a body-soul composite.[148] Yet, if we would do justice to Paul, the concept of bodily resurrection should not be interpreted so vaguely that it loses all corporeal implications. For instance, Willi Marxsen, pp. 69-70, would regard Paul's reference to "body" as no more than a reference to the personal "I," so that resurrection for Paul need have meant no more than the continuity of the "I" from one mode of existence to another. But for Paul there is more than a continuity of personal existence—in resurrection there is a continuity of the corporeal aspect of personal existence. (And so the modern suggestion that in resurrection the body may corrupt and the person still goes on, while it may involve a continuity of the "I," would not convey Paul's idea of the corporality of the "I.")

On the other hand it is clear that Paul does not conceive of the risen "body" in a merely physical way. His comments make us wonder whether he would be in agreement with Luke (who was not an eyewitness of the risen Jesus) about the properties of the risen body. Certainly, from Paul's description one would never suspect that a risen body could eat, as Luke reports. Moreover, Paul distinguishes between the risen body that can enter heaven and "flesh and blood" that cannot enter heaven— a distinction that does not agree with the emphasis in Luke 24:39 on the "flesh and bones" of the risen Jesus.

Perhaps a digression on this point would not be out of place, for it is of major importance to a solution of the problem we are discussing. Most modern scholars maintain that,

---

resurrection (cf. also Philip 1:21-23) and so may be a poor guide to what resurrection involves. Finally, we should remember that while I Cor 15 implies a general analogy between the resurrection of the Christian and the resurrection of Jesus, Paul must face problems about the earthly bodies of Christians that did not arise about the earthly body of Jesus—their bodies will have decomposed or have been lost by the time of the general resurrection of the just, whereas Jesus was raised "on the third day."

[148] For a brief summary of the complex problem of Pauline anthropology see J. A. Fitzmyer, *The Jerome Biblical Commentary* (n. 2 above), art. 79, §§117-23.

by way of apologetics against those who would deny a bodily resurrection, some of the evangelists, especially Luke and John, have presented too physical a picture of the risen Jesus.[149] Does this not imply that an inspired evangelist is employing a falsified argument? Fundamentalists often claim that if one does not give full consent to the Lucan view of a risen Jesus who can be touched and who can eat, one has undermined the credibility of all the NT evidence for a bodily resurrection. But the terminology "true" and "false" should not be simplistically applied here for several reasons: (a) It is one thing to posit that the evangelists created a picture they knew to be inaccurate in order to confute their opponents; it is another thing to say that they reported an already existing picture of the risen Jesus, a picture of whose detailed accuracy they did not have control. Since the idea of Jesus' eating and of having his wounds probed appears in Luke and in John, it was probably a tradition anterior to both.[150] (b) Some of the objectification of the body

---

[149] In evaluating this picture, perhaps we should distinguish in likelihood between a risen body being touched and a risen body eating. Paul rejects elements of corruptibility in the risen body; those elements are clearly involved in eating, but not so clearly involved in being touched (or being seen). By way of more general comment, Benoit, a moderate critic, admits (p. 285) the apologetic interest of the Lucan account but maintains that this does not diminish its historicity. He contends that Luke does not mean that glorified bodies needed food but only that Jesus accommodated himself to the disciples' understanding and gave them a proof that he could eat and was no mere phantom. I am not sure that this observation really answers the objection raised to Luke's account on the basis of the Pauline evidence. Nevertheless, it is certainly beyond Luke's intention to have Christians debating as to whether what Jesus ate was glorified as part of his body or somehow never became part of him.

[150] Ignatius, *Smyrnaeans*, 3:2-3, narrates that when Jesus came to Peter and his companions, he invited them to lay hold and handle him, saying, "See that I am not a demon without a body"; and they did so. We note that the objectification of Jesus has gone further than in the Gospels—they actually touch him. Some think that in this story Ignatius is not dependent upon Luke but preserves a variant, parallel tradition.

of the risen Jesus is the proper work of the individual evangelist. For example, Luke has the risen Jesus spend several hours walking and chatting with the disciples on the road to Emmaus; John 21 has him prepare a fire and food. These details may reflect the artistry of effective narration, for they appear precisely in the Gospels of the two most accomplished narrators among the evangelists.[151] We should note too that Luke has a special tendency to objectivize the supernatural. All the Gospels tell of the divine spirit descending as a dove upon Jesus at the time of his baptism, but only Luke 3:22 reports that this was "in a bodily form." (c) While the Lucan and Johannine stories imply a rather physical understanding of what has occurred in the raising of Jesus' body, their main interest is not in the physical properties of the body as such—they are emphasizing the corporeal continuity between the earthly and the risen Jesus. If we accept the implication of I Cor 15:44 that Jesus' risen body was corporeal but not natural or physical *(psychikos)*, it is not surprising that the Gospel stories, written with another main interest, use too broad a brush stroke in trying to capture in a narrative such a basically indescribable eschatological reality. (d) The same two evangelists, Luke and John, supply a counteractive to a crass physical understanding by having the disciples fail to recognize the risen Jesus (Luke 24:16; John 20:14; 21:4) and by describing Jesus as exempt from the usual laws of space (Luke 24:31; John 20:19, 26).[152]

Returning to I Cor 15 and accepting the less-physical Pauline description of the body of the risen Jesus, we may wonder whether the ultimate implication of Paul's remarks is not to

---

[151] As we shall see, there are different types of appearance narratives in the Gospels, some being more circumstantial than others, especially in describing how Jesus was recognized. There is nothing in the Roman Catholic notion of biblical inspiration that would forbid the suggestion that those responsible for the resurrection narratives employed the techniques of dramatization. See p. 19 above on literary form.

[152] The strange scene in John 20:17 where Jesus tells Magdalene, "Do not cling to me," may be a dramatization of the theological truth that Jesus has not returned to ordinary existence but rather to a glorified existence with his Father.

reduce the appearances of the risen Jesus to purely internal experiences.[153] Much depends on how we understand the word "appeared" in I Cor 15:5 (also Luke 24:34; Acts 13:31). It is a translation of the Greek *ōphthē,* a passive form of the verb "to see." The dative construction employed with the verb suggests a translation "appeared to," rather than "was seen by."[154] A study of this verb in the Greek Bible shows that it covers a wide range of visual experience including contacts with supernatural beings such as God and angels, so that it does not have to imply physical sight.[155] Therefore, we cannot simply *assume* that when

---

[153] It is worth noting that, in listing six persons or groups to whom the risen Jesus appeared, Paul makes no distinction about types of appearances. He regards the appearance to himself on the same level as the appearance to the others, even if it is the last. This differs from Luke's evaluation of the experience granted to Paul; for in Acts Luke distinguishes sharply between Jesus' appearances "to the apostles whom he had chosen" (1:2) during forty days before his ascension and the experience of Saul on the road to Damascus which took place considerably later. To the apostles Jesus appeared in a remarkably tangible way, but it was a light from heaven that flashed or shone around Saul (9:3; 22:6; 26:13). One could even get the impression from Acts that Paul did not see Jesus but only heard the voice that came from heaven (where Jesus is at the right hand of the Father—see 7:55). However, that is probably not Luke's intention, for in Acts 9:17 Ananias speaks of Jesus' having *appeared* to Paul and in 26:16 Jesus says to Paul, "For this purpose I *appeared* to you to appoint you a minister and witness both of these things wherein you have *seen* me and wherein I will appear to you." Note that the same combination of "see" and "appear" occurs in I Cor 9:1 and 15:8, two passages where Paul describes his own experience.

[154] Evans, p. 64. Similarly a passive form of the verb *phaneroun,* having the idea of "being made manifest," is employed to describe an encounter with the risen Jesus in the Marcan Appendix 16:12, 14 and in John 21:14 (cf. also "Jesus manifested himself" in John 21:1). An aorist passive of *phainein,* "appear," occurs in the Marcan Appendix 16:9.

[155] It is dubious, however, how much of the OT usage really refers to non-physical sight. When, for instance, Gen 12:7 records that God appeared to Abraham, the author may be thinking of God's appearing in a human form, precisely the form in which he could be seen by the eye of man. When I Tim 3:16 says that Jesus,

Paul speaks of Jesus "appearing" to him or when he says that he "saw" Jesus (I Cor 9:1),[156] he means physical sight of a corporeal being. It is noteworthy that elsewhere he refers to his experience in terms of God's having *revealed* His Son to him— "revelation" is a less physical term, although it would not exclude external sight.[157] Nevertheless, the overall evidence does not favor the thesis that Paul was describing a purely internal experience, for he speaks of Jesus' having appeared to more than 500 at once (I Cor 15:6); and we can scarcely think of synchronized ecstasy. (This observation holds true no matter where Paul got the information about this appearance; for Paul, who himself saw the risen Jesus, found no contradiction in

---

victorious over death, appeared to the angels, we must remember that in the Jewish imagination the angels had a (male) bodily form —they were circumcised; they could beget children, etc. Thus a type of physical sight may be meant.

[156] The language of "seeing" the risen Jesus is more frequent in the Gospels than is the language of his "appearing": Mark 16:7; Matt 28:17; Luke 24:37, 39; John 20:18, 25, 29; Marcan Appendix 16:11. The partial ambiguity of our sources about the nature of "seeing" makes incredible some of the modern speculation as to whether the risen Jesus could have been photographed or televised, and whether he could have been seen by non-believers. This type of question does not show any appreciation for the transformation involved in the resurrection.

[157] There is little basis for Marxsen's suspicion (p. 105) that earlier Paul described his experience as "revelation" and only later began to use "seeing" or "appearance" by concession to and assimilation with the common usage. The same chapter of Galatians that speaks of God's "revealing" His Son to Paul (1:16) speaks of His raising Jesus from the dead (1:1), without the slightest sign of tension between the two ideas.

Léon-Dufour, pp. 88-92, thinks he has found still another example of alternative Pauline vocabulary for describing the encounter with the risen Jesus: "the surpassing *knowledge [gnōsis]* of my Lord Jesus Christ" (Philip 3:8). "Knowledge" would be much less physical in its implication than "seeing"; but it is not at all clear that this passage (or others that Léon-Dufour cites as examples) refers to the encounter with the risen Jesus mentioned in I Cor 15:8. It may be a reference to Paul's subsequent reflections on that encounter.

positing that what happened to him could have happened to
500 people at the same time.) How are we to reconcile a "sight"
that is not necessarily physical and to be seen by all with an
appearance that is not purely internal?[158] We find that the idea
of sight/appearance in Paul's description of the risen Jesus is
just as paradoxical as the idea of a body that is corporeal but
spiritual (not *psychikos*). In short, our language of space-time
experience breaks down when it is used to describe the eschatological.

(2) *Paul's list of the recipients of the appearances.* Having
seen the difficulties of interpreting the implications in the Corinthian formula with its sequence of death, burial, resurrection,
and appearance(s), let us now turn to the list of six recipients
(I Cor 15:5b-8) that Paul himself seemingly added to the
primitive formula. Obviously, even if Paul is the actual com-
poser of the list, he is dependent on tradition for the information
about those to whom Jesus appeared. Perhaps he got this information when he went to Jerusalem after his conversion and saw
Cephas and James (Gal 1:18-19), both of whom are mentioned
in the list.

Since our next area of discussion in this chapter will be the
Gospel narratives of the appearances of the risen Jesus, it may
be useful here to investigate whether or not it is possible to
correlate the Pauline list with the Gospel appearances. The
latter are localized, either in the Jerusalem area or in Galilee;
Paul says nothing about where the appearances occurred. The
fact that our earliest written evidence does not localize the ap-

---

[158] Fuller, p. 33, is willing to describe the events as visionary but
not as visions. Even though Paul says he saw the risen Lord, Fuller,
pp. 46-48, very tentatively proposes that Luke is right in saying that
Paul saw a light, and he calls attention to II Cor 4:6: God "has
shone in our hearts to give the light of the knowledge of the glory
of God in the face of Christ." Thus, for Fuller the "appearances"
of the risen Jesus "involved visionary experiences of light, combined
with a communication of meaning." Personally I would not agree
that the Pauline evidence points in this direction, and I think that
even the understanding of the Lucan evidence is dubious (see n.
153 above).

pearances raises the possibility that the variant Gospel localizations (a variance that is a real problem, as we shall see) may stem, in part at least, not from a historical tradition but from the evangelists' attempts to supply a setting.

Similarly the Gospel narratives of appearances have chronological indications, e.g., Easter Sunday evening; a week later; etc. Moreover, as befits a consecutive account, Jesus appears to some witnesses (Mary Magdalene or the disciples on the road to Emmaus) before he appears to others (the Twelve). What about Paul's list—is it in chronological order? He explicitly refers to himself as last, and he may well imply that Cephas was the first among the better known companions of Jesus to be favored with an appearance. (The priority of the appearance to Cephas would agree with Luke 24:34[159] and would help to explain Peter's importance in the early Church.) Some have thought that chronological order can be found throughout the list by identifying the appearances mentioned by Paul with those narrated in the Gospels and Acts, thus: [1] "to Cephas" with Luke 24:34; [2] "then to the Twelve" with Luke 24:36 (see vs. 33); [3] "then to more than 500 brethren at one time" with the Pentecost scene in Acts 2. The attempted identifications become even more fanciful after [3] because there is no other NT mention of an appearance to James [4]. The forced character of these identifications is clear when we recall that Luke, the author of Acts, did not consider the Pentecost scene an appearance of the risen Jesus, for he describes it after Jesus has ascended into heaven, terminating the forty days in which he appeared to his chosen apostles (Acts 1:2-3). Moreover, the number of people that Luke mentions in the context of the Pentecost scene (Acts 1:15) is 120 not 500.

---

[159] Marxsen, p. 58, attempts to find an alternative form of the tradition of an appearance to Peter in John 20:3-10: "We are certainly intended to suppose that Peter (who, according to the account, was first inside the tomb) also believed." This is not certain at all, since John tells us only that the Beloved Disciple believed, and he is contrasted with Peter. The Johannine story is a variant of the empty tomb narrative, not a variant of an appearance narrative.

Most scholars despair of cross-identification and propose that the arrangement in Paul's list of six appearances is logical rather than chronological. The list breaks easily into two groupings of three. It has been suggested that the first three appearances (Cephas, the Twelve, 500 brethren) were to those who had followed Jesus during his lifetime, while the second group of three appearances (James, all the apostles, Paul) were directed to new followers of Jesus.[160] Another explanation (that can be complementary) is that the first group of appearances were Church-founding, for Peter, the Twelve, and the Pentecost Christians were involved in the establishment of the earliest Jerusalem community; and the second group of appearances were mission-inaugurating appearances, for James, the apostles and Paul were responsible for the missionary spread of Christianity.[161] This explanation limps because of the dubious iden-

---

[160] In describing James, "the brother of the Lord" (Gal 1:19), as a *new* follower of Jesus, I am accepting the common scholarly opinion that this James is not to be identified with either of the two Jameses who are named in the Lucan lists of the Twelve (Luke 6:13-16; Acts 1:13), to wit, James of Zebedee and James of Alphaeus; for Luke explicitly distinguishes the Twelve from the brothers of Jesus (Acts 1:14). These brothers or relatives are portrayed in the ministry as unbelievers (John 7:5). In describing "the apostles" as *new* followers of Jesus, I am assuming that for Paul the term apostle covered a wider group than the Twelve; it was a designation of those who were sent out to preach the resurrection. This Pauline understanding of "apostle" differed from the Lucan understanding whereby the Twelve are always the apostles par excellence. For detail see R. E. Brown, *Priest and Bishop* (New York: Paulist, 1970), pp. 48-51, 60-63.

[161] This theory is advanced by Fuller, pp. 34-48. While I agree that both Church-founding and mission elements were in the commission given by the risen Jesus, I am dubious that the appearances can be divided according to these two thrusts (of what I would regard as the one basic commission). That his division is highly imaginative becomes patent when Fuller tells us (p. 38) to think of James as "the chairman of the central board of missions," inaugurating the mission outside Jerusalem. It was the Hellenist Christians, not James, who inaugurated this mission, according to Acts chs. 6-8.

tification of the 500 with the Pentecost Christians and because we have no evidence that James played a missionary role.

Still another approach is that Paul's list was made up from two separate reports. One report was that the risen Jesus had appeared to Cephas and to the Twelve; the other report was that he had appeared to James and to the apostles. These two reports were regarded by A. von Harnack as "rival" in the sense that they were circulated by followers of Peter and James respectively.[162] E. Bammel has suggested that they were duplicate reports of the same appearances, with James substituted for Cephas, and the apostles substituted for the Twelve. This is unlikely: Paul was well informed about the main characters of the Jerusalem church and was in a position to know whether there were traditions that Jesus had appeared both to Peter and to James. An appearance to Peter has independent support in the NT; and one must probably postulate an appearance to James[163] to account for the fact that a disbelieving brother of the Lord became a leading Christian.

All this debate indicates how difficult it is to make any judgments, not only about the geography of the appearances listed by Paul, but also about their chronology.[164] It increases

---

[162] The theory that Peter was replaced by James as the head of the (Jerusalem) church is sometimes deduced from the shift in the order in which the names Cephas and James appear in Gal 1:18-19 (Cephas first) and 2:9 (James first, Cephas second). The deduction is very questionable, and the whole theory does not do justice to the different roles of Peter and of James at Jerusalem. Peter probably never was the head of the local Jerusalem church. As the first of the Twelve he was a dominant figure there; but from the moment that the local church was large and complex enough to need regular administration (as indicated by Acts 6:1-4), the role of administrator was not played by one of the Twelve but by James and the presbyters, at least for the Hebrew Christians. For details and bibliography concerning the "two-report" approach to the Pauline list of appearances see Evans, pp. 43ff.; Fuller, pp. 11ff.

[163] Such an appearance is reported in fragment 7 of *The Gospel of the Hebrews,* an early second-century Jewish Christian composition.

[164] Nor can we solve the problem of what a second appearance of the risen Jesus might have meant to the recipient, e.g., if Cephas

the likelihood that the variations among the Gospel narratives
of the appearances arose in part because there never was one
unanimously accepted tradition with a complete geographical
or chronological sequence of appearances.[165]

III. The Gospel Narratives of the
Appearances to the Twelve

We are now ready to turn from early formulas or procla-

(Peter) were present again when Jesus appeared to the Twelve, or
if the Twelve were present again when Jesus appeared to "all the
apostles." The appearances may have had different purposes: to
bring the recipient to faith, to commission him or them, etc. I
would reject as hypercriticism Marxsen's attempt (pp. 89-90) to
reduce the Pauline list *ad absurdum* by dwelling on the problem
of these possible duplications, as well as his argument (also p. 99)
that only the appearance to Peter was constitutive for faith. Consequently I find minimalistic his contention that historical evidence
shows only that Peter was the first to believe, and not that Peter
was the first to see the risen Jesus.

[165] Probably individual Christian communities had independent
reminiscences of particular appearances of the risen Jesus, and a
passage like I Cor 15:5-8 is an example of one attempt to collect
some of these reminiscences. V. Taylor, *The Formation of the
Gospel Tradition* (London: Macmillan, 1935), pp. 59-62, has
pointed out why the story of the post-resurrectional events would
take form differently from the story of the passion and would not
necessarily emerge in uniform sequence. The details of the passion
would be meaningless unless from the start they were fitted into a
sequence leading from arrest to crucifixion. One could scarcely tell
of the arrest of Jesus without telling of the outcome; the sentencing
had to precede the execution, etc. But the post-resurrection appearances were first reported to root Christian faith in the risen Jesus
and to justify the apostolic preaching. To do this it would be
enough to report one or two appearances of Jesus and not necessary to supply a chain of these appearances. And obviously the
appearances that were reported would be those made to the more
important figures known by Christians, for example, Peter, the
Twelve, and James. The principal Palestinian communities of Jerusalem and Galilee might retain the memory of appearances that
were important to them because of local associations.

mations of resurrection faith to those consecutive Gospel narratives describing the post-resurrectional happenings. There are two general types: narratives of how women (and others) came to the tomb of Jesus and found it empty, and narratives of the appearance of Jesus to those who had known him during his lifetime. In a certain sense the appearance narratives are less germane to our inquiry about the bodily resurrection and could be treated quickly—especially since we have already (pp. 87-92 above) evaluated their manner of describing the risen Jesus (how he could be touched, how he ate, etc.). Yet, at least as regards their sequence, the appearance narratives must be discussed; for, as we have just seen, the Pauline list of appearances offers little guidance on this point. The Gospels give the impression of a close sequence between the discovery of the empty tomb and the appearance of Jesus. Moreover, a connection is made between the two events through the medium of angels who appear at the empty tomb to explain that Jesus has been raised and will appear. If that was the real order of events, there could never have been an early Christian faith in Jesus' victory over death that did not involve bodily resurrection against the background of the empty tomb. But critical scholarship has taught us that the sequence was not so simple.

(A) General Critical Suppositions

Before we can deal with the Gospel narratives, clarity is required about three suppositions of biblical criticism that affect our procedure. *First,* the verses that conclude the Gospel of Mark in most bibles (Mark 16:9-20, called the Marcan Appendix or the Longer Ending of Mark) were not the original ending of the Gospel but were added because of the abrupt termination in 16:8.[166] (Scholars are divided on whether Mark

---

[166] The Marcan Appendix is missing in Codices Vaticanus and Sinaiticus. Minor textual witnesses of Mark preserve for us other attempts at completing the Gospel (two of which are translated in *The New American Bible*). Roman Catholics regard the Marcan

originally terminated with 16:8 or whether there was a further
narrative that was lost—I favor the former opinion.) The date
of the Marcan Appendix is difficult to determine precisely, but
it is later than that of the other Gospel accounts. Some scholars
attribute no importance to the evidence of the Appendix about
the resurrection, for they think of it as a secondary reshuffling
of material already found in the canonical Gospels (it is closest
to Luke and Matthew). But a close vocabulary comparison
suggests that, at least in part, the writer of the Appendix may
have drawn on sources similar to the canonical Gospels rather
than on the Gospels themselves;[167] and so it is worth while in
our comparisons to include information taken from the Appendix. In what follows "Mark" refers to Mark 16:1-8, and we
shall refer to the remaining verses of Mark 16 as the Marcan
Appendix.

Second, the resurrection narrative in Luke 24 contains verses
(3, 6, 9, 12, 36, 40, 51, and 52) that are textually dubious in
whole or in part. These verses are found in the majority of
important textual witnesses but are regularly absent from Codex
Bezae and from the Itala form of the Old Latin (late second-
century) translation—two Western witnesses to the Gospel text
that are usually characterized by interpolations or additions
rather than by omissions. The absence of these verses in the
very type of Western witnesses that one would have expected
to contain them has earned for them the peculiarly negative
designation of "Western Noninterpolations." Although it was
fashionable in the early part of the century to dismiss these
verses as scribal additions, their presence in the recently discovered second-century papyrus P[75] had made many rethink
this position.[168] The latest critical editions of the Greek NT
(the second edition of the United Bible Societies, and the forthcoming 26th edition of Nestle) have accepted these verses as

---

Appendix as canonical Scripture, which means that it is inspired
but not necessarily a part of the original Gospel of Mark.

[167] See Fuller, pp. 156-57.

[168] K. Snodgrass, " 'Western Non-Interpolations,' " *Journal of
Biblical Literature* 91 (1972), 369-79.

part of the authentic text of Luke's Gospel. In any case, we shall consider them in collecting evidence about the resurrection, although the reader is reminded of the textual problem.

Third, there is scholarly agreement that ch. 21 of John was written by someone other than the evangelist who was responsible for the body of the Gospel. It represents Johannine tradition added to the Gospel by a redactor (perhaps a disciple of the evangelist),[169] and its witness to the post-resurrectional appearances is different from and independent of the witness preserved in ch. 20.

As a result of these critical suppositions we may speak of six Gospel accounts as sources for our knowledge of the resurrection. In an accompanying chart I summarize the evidence from these accounts in reference to the narratives of the post-resurrectional appearances.

(B) The Sequence of the Appearances

It is quite obvious from a glance at the chart that the Gospels do not agree as to where and to whom Jesus appeared after his resurrection. Mark mentions no appearance of Jesus, although 16:7 indicates that Peter and his disciples will see him in Galilee. Matthew mentions an appearance to the women in Jerusalem (28:9-10) that seemingly contradicts the instruction to go to Galilee where Jesus will be seen (28:7). The main appearance for Matthew is in Galilee when Jesus is seen by the Eleven disciples on a mountain (28:16-20). Luke narrates several appearances in the Jerusalem area: to the two disciples on the road to Emmaus (24:13-32), to Simon (34), and to the Eleven and others gathered together in Jerusalem (36-53). All of these are described by Luke as having taken place on the same day, Easter itself; and Jesus is pictured as finally departing from his disciples (to heaven—Western Noninterpolation of 51) on Easter night (yet see the contradictory information in Acts

---

[169] For detail see R. E. Brown, *The Gospel According to John, XIII-XXI* (Garden City, N. Y.: Doubleday, 1970), pp. 1077-80.

THE VARIANT GOSPEL NARRATIVES OF THE POST-RESURRECTIONAL APPEARANCES*

	Mark 16:1-8	Matt 28	Luke 24	Mark 16:9-20	John 20	John 21
Tomb Area		To women returning from tomb / They clasped his feet / He repeated message about Galilee		First to Mary Magdalene	At tomb to Mary Magdalene / "Don't cling to me" / He spoke of ascending	
			To Simon (vs. 34)			
Country Road			To two disciples on road to Emmaus	To two of them walking in the country		
Jerusalem			To Eleven / At meal Easter night	To Eleven / At table Afterwards	To disciples minus Thomas, one of the Twelve / At meal Easter night / To disciples with Thomas Week later	
Galilee	See promise in 16:7	To Eleven On a mountain				To seven disciples At Sea of Tiberias

*This chart and the chart on p. 118, along with short sections of the accompanying discussion, are taken with permission from my Anchor volume Bible *The Gospel According to John, XIII-XXI* (pp. 968-974), copyright 1970 by Doubleday and Co., Inc.

1:3). In John 20, as in Luke, there are appearances in the Jerusalem area: to Mary Magdalene (20:14-18), to the disciples without Thomas (19-23), and to the disciples with Thomas a week later (26-29). In John 21 there is an appearance to seven disciples in Galilee at the Sea of Tiberias. Finally, in the Marcan Appendix there is a set of appearances, all seemingly in the Jerusalem area: to Mary Magdalene (16:9), to two disciples in the country (12-13), and to the Eleven at table (14-19).

If we concentrate on the appearances to the Twelve,[170] we find that in three accounts (Luke, John 20, Marcan Appendix) Jesus appears to them gathered together in a room or at table in *Jerusalem.* In two accounts (Matthew and John 21), and possibly by implication in Mark 16:7, Jesus appears to them in *Galilee,* either on a mountain, or at the Sea of Tiberias. How are we to decide which tradition is the oldest and where Jesus first appeared? The Twelve were the official witnesses of the risen Jesus, and their preaching shaped resurrection faith. Obviously if Jesus appeared to them in Jerusalem immediately after the discovery of the empty tomb, this sequence is important for the idea of bodily resurrection.

The usual way to harmonize the Gospel variations is to

---

[170] I use the expression "the Twelve" which Paul uses in I Cor 15:5. Actually Judas had left the group, so that "the Eleven" would be more exact (as in Matt 28:16 and Luke 24:33), or even "the Ten" in the instance of John 20:19-23 where "Thomas, one of the Twelve" was absent (20:24). I do not intend to discuss at any length the problem of the "minor" appearances of Jesus to Mary Magdalene (and other women) and to the disciples on the road to Emmaus, for the recipients of these appearances were not official witnesses and so apparently did not shape the resurrection faith of the early community. (For instance, Marcan Appendix 16:11 reports that no credence was given to Mary Magdalene.) The omission of these minor appearances in Paul's Corinthian list does not necessarily imply that the tradition of such appearances was not historical or was a late development, as some scholars would argue. The claim that the risen Jesus appeared first to Cephas means that *among those who would testify publicly* Peter was the first to see Jesus. It would not exclude an earlier appearance to Magdalene.

posit that Jesus appeared at least twice to the Twelve, first on Easter Sunday night in Jerusalem, then sometime later in Galilee. In part, this sequence arises from the Fourth Gospel, the one Gospel that has both Jerusalem and Galilee appearances to members of the Twelve. However, as we saw in discussing critical suppositions, the present Johannine order is thought to result from the work of a redactor who appended a chapter of Galilean appearances to an already formed Gospel. Thus the order of Jerusalem appearances (John 20) and Galilee appearances (John 21) tells us nothing about the actual course of events. In fact, when studied carefully, the Gospel evidence makes a Jerusalem-to-Galilee sequence most unlikely.

Let us look first at the Gospel accounts that localize the appearance(s) to the Twelve in *Jerusalem*. In John 20 the two appearances take place over an eight-day period (vss. 19, 26). The words of Jesus to Thomas give the clear impression that the second appearance is a finale, and the evangelist heightens this impression by supplying an ending for the Gospel (20:30-31) immediately after the Thomas scene. Nothing here would encourage the reader to expect further appearances to the Twelve in Galilee.

The situation is even clearer in Luke. Jesus appears to the Twelve on Easter Sunday night. At the end of the appearance (Luke 24:50) we are told that Jesus led them out of Jerusalem as far as Bethany and departed from them (vs. 51), ascending into heaven (Western Noninterpolation of vs. 51). One gets the same picture in the Marcan Appendix 16:7. No room whatsoever is left for subsequent Galilean appearances. Indeed, a study of how Luke (24:6) changes the import of Mark 16:7 indicates a desire on Luke's part to erase any mention of appearances in Galilee.

True, in Acts 1:3 Luke shows an awareness of a longer period of post-resurrectional appearances. But even in Acts there is no mention of Galilean appearances, and the ascension after forty days takes place in the Jerusalem area (1:12). In fact, the information in Acts raises acutely questions about the historicity of the whole Lucan schema. How are we to reconcile what is said at the end of the Gospel (departure/ascension on

Easter Sunday night) and what is said at the beginning of Acts (ascension forty days later)?[171] In Acts the ascension is preparatory to the scene of the coming of the Spirit of Pentecost which is meant to have the emphasis, for Pentecost marks the beginning of the missionary thrust of Christianity that Luke will describe in the book. Realizing this primacy of Pentecost, we can interpret the first chapter of Acts as a Lucan attempt to fill in the time between two datable events, approximately fifty days apart: Jesus' death at Passover time and the charismatic manifestation at Pentecost. By allotting definite spans of time to the events surrounding the resurrection (appearances, glorification, giving of the Spirit) Luke is able to provide a bridge between the earthly ministry of Jesus and the history of the Christian community.

Luke's guiding motive was theological, but we can see that he was working with earlier data when he was constructing this chronological schema. *First,* the early Christians seemingly had a tradition concerning a certain period of time in which the risen Jesus appeared to men and after which the appearances ceased. In I Cor 15:8 Paul speaks of Jesus having appeared to him "last of all"—a statement that implies that by A.D. 56 (when Paul wrote I Corinthians) he had not heard of any appearances having taken place since Jesus had appeared to him twenty years before (mid-30's).[172] Since the conversion of

---

[171] To solve the problem it has been suggested that Luke did not write Acts 1:1-5, but that it was the awkward composition of an unknown Christian scribe, necessitated when Luke-Acts, originally one book, was split into two. The scribe, supposedly, wrote an introduction for the second book by imitating the style of the introduction to the first (cf. Luke 1:3 and Acts 1:1). Another suggestion is that Luke the theologian wrote one way when terminating the Gospel-story of Jesus, while Luke the would-be historian wrote another way when beginning the Acts-story of the Church. By associating exaltation or ascension more closely with resurrection, the Gospel was truer to the original theological understanding of the resurrection, while Acts divided resurrection from ascension in order to make both a part of a continuous story.

[172] This indication means that Paul attributed a unique character to the appearances of the risen Jesus—for him they were not iden-

Paul did not take place till three to six years after Easter, Paul's inclusion of himself in a list of appearances implies a much longer period of post-resurrectional appearances than has normally been conceded. In Acts Luke marks off the period of appearances as forty days, seemingly with the purpose of drawing attention to the parallels between Christian origins and the origins of Israel with whom God made a covenant during their stay of *forty* years in the desert. This interpretation of Lucan thought is supported by the fact that motifs of the covenant, the exodus, and the desert life abound in Acts' description of the origins and life of the early Jerusalem community.

Second, it seems that in primitive Christian theology Jesus' ascension into heaven (his glorification) and his communication of the Spirit were understood as aspects of the resurrection of Jesus, constituting with it one eschatological act of God.[173] The union of these ideas may have been suggested by the fact that the Lord who appeared to the disciples was Jesus *exalted* in glory; and from this appearance the disciples came to understand that Jesus had been *raised* from the dead, as they felt the presence of his *Spirit* in their lives. Evidence for this is found, for instance, in Matt 28:18 where the risen Jesus appears endowed with all the power of heaven—clearly he has already ascended to God's right hand. Passages like Acts 3:13; 5:30-31; Eph 1:20; and I Peter 1:21 interpret resurrection in the language of glorification, exaltation, and ascension. John 20:22 has the risen Jesus confer the Holy Spirit on the occasion of his first appearance to the disciples on Easter Sunday night. Luke is correct, then, in including ascension and the giving of the Spirit in the resurrectional era; but by separating them over a period of forty and fifty days he chooses to describe the escha-

---

tical with Jesus' continued presence through the Spirit in the Church and in the Christian, nor with his presence in the Christian mission and proclamation.

[173] For the ascension see Benoit, pp. 334, 341-42; also his article in *Theology Digest* 8 (1960), 105-10; A. M. Ramsey, "What Was the Ascension?" in *Historicity and Chronology in the New Testament,* ed. M. C. Perry (Theological Collections 6; London: SPCK, 1965), pp. 135-44.

tological in the categories of time.[174] And so, despite the fact that the Jerusalem tradition of post-resurrectional appearances (especially Luke-Acts) draws on early data, it cannot be followed in determining the real sequence of those appearances.

Is the *Galilean* tradition of appearances chronologically more reliable then? Just as the Jerusalem tradition leaves little or no room for subsequent Galilean appearances, the Galilean narratives seem to rule out any prior appearances of Jesus to the Twelve in Jerusalem. The angel's directive in Mark 16:7 and Matt 28:7 bids the disciples to go to Galilee to see Jesus— a command that would make little sense were they to see him first in Jerusalem! When Jesus does appear to the disciples on the mountain in Galilee (Matt 28:16-17), they express doubt; and such hesitancy is elsewhere associated with initial appearances (Luke 24:37; John 20:25; Mark 16:13, 14). There would be no reason for doubt if the disciples had already seen Jesus in Jerusalem and knew of his resurrection. The redactor who added ch. 21 to the Fourth Gospel tried to adapt his account of an appearance in Galilee to the preceding account (John 20) where the appearances were in Jerusalem. He smoothed out the sequence by adding time indications: e.g., "Jesus manifested himself *again*" (21:1), and "This was now the *third time* that Jesus was manifested to his disciples" (21:14). But this redactional patchwork does not disguise the

---

[174] Indeed he even employs the categories of space. Exaltation at God's right hand and the giving of the Spirit are theological concepts, but Luke has brought them into the realm of the sensible by portraying Jesus lifted up on a cloud that takes him out of sight, and by describing a mighty gust of spirit-wind (the one Hebrew word *rûah* can be rendered "spirit" and "wind") sweeping down from heaven. While Luke has attempted to describe the ascension and the giving of the Spirit, no NT author attempted to describe the resurrection itself. Our earliest recorded attempt to do this is in the second-century *Gospel of Peter* 39-40: "They saw again three men come out from the sepulcher, two of them sustaining the other, and a cross following them. The heads of the two reached to heaven, but the head of him whom they led by the hand outreached the heavens."

fact that in the story of ch. 21 the disciples are seeing the risen Jesus for the first time (21:4, 7, 12).

Thus we must reject the thesis that the Gospels can be harmonized through a rearrangement whereby Jesus appears several times to the Twelve, first in Jerusalem, then in Galilee. As Bishop Descamps argued persuasively some years ago,[175] the different Gospel accounts are narrating, so far as substance is concerned, the *same* basic appearance to the Twelve, whether they locate it in Jerusalem or in Galilee—an appearance that is all important for the Church since through it the Twelve are commissioned for their future task.

The puzzled reader may well ask: How can such diverse Gospel accounts all refer to the same appearance to the Twelve? We have already seen that variations in place and time may stem in part from the evangelists themselves who are trying to fit the account of an appearance into a consecutive narrative.[176] If one lays aside such minor details, there is a general similarity of pattern in the Gospel accounts of this appearance of Jesus to the Twelve:[177]

---

[175] A. Descamps, "La structure des récits évangéliques de la résurrection," *Biblica* 40 (1959), 726-41. It is interesting that one of the first Catholic attempts to apply trenchant biblical criticism to the post-resurrectional narratives would be by a scholar who would become a bishop and a member of the Pontifical Biblical Commission.

[176] Other features in the Gospel accounts may also represent the theological outlook of the evangelists. For instance, only John reports that Thomas was absent when Jesus appeared to the Twelve, and so John has Jesus appear to Thomas a week later. In my commentary on John (n. 169 above), pp. 1031-33, I suggest that this second appearance may be the evangelist's dramatization in which Thomas serves to personify an attitude. The other Gospels mention fright or disbelief when Jesus appears, but John transferred this doubt to a separate episode and personified it in Thomas. Such free dramatization is characteristic of the Fourth Gospel.

[177] An important analysis of the patterns of the narratives is offered by C. H. Dodd, "The Appearances of the Risen Christ: An Essay in Form-Criticism of the Gospels," in *Studies in the Gospels*, ed. D. E. Nineham (R. H. Lightfoot volume; Oxford Univ. Press,

(1) A situation is described in which Jesus' followers are bereft of him.

(2) The appearance of Jesus.

(3) His greeting to his followers.

(4) Their recognition of him.

(5) His word of command or mission.

For the purposes of this chapter a great difficulty arises from the fact that the commands of the risen Jesus to the Twelve, as recorded in the Gospels, while similar in intent, are quite different in their wording. The reader should carefully compare Matt 28:18-20; Luke 24:47-49; John 20:21-23; and Marcan Appendix 16:15-18. He will find in these commands motifs of mission to the world, of preaching and teaching, of the forgiveness of sins, of baptism, and of the giving of the promised Holy Spirit. But each Gospel phrases these motifs very differently and often in a style characteristic of the respective evangelist.[178] In the instance of the "Trinitarian" baptismal formula of Matt 28:19 even moderate scholars would admit that we have a phrasing that can scarcely stem from the first days of Christianity.[179] This observation brings us face to face with the problem of whether the risen Jesus communicated with words,[180] or was there some type of intuitive communication by Jesus that found words only later in the various traditions? It is not

---

1957), pp. 9-35. The two patterns he distinguishes are Concise Narratives and Circumstantial Narratives. (Benoit prefers another designation: narratives that contain a mission and narratives that contain a recognition). The pattern given above is the Concise Narrative. In the Circumstantial Narratives the details of the recognition are more developed.

[178] Evans, p. 67, phrases the difficulty concisely: ". . . that not only does the Lord not say the same things in any two Gospels, but that it is hardly the same Lord who speaks. In Matthew it is evidently a Matthean Lord who speaks, in Luke a Lukan Lord and in John a Johannine Lord."

[179] Benoit, pp. 337-38, "Matthew would have written down the baptismal words in the formula used in his day [about A.D. 70-80]."

[180] Notice the self-contradictory character of the Lucan information in Acts 9:7 and 22:9 about whether or not those who were with Paul on the road to Damascus heard a heavenly voice.

a question that can be decided with certitude. If there were words, they must have consisted of a general missionary mandate that was subsequently formulated differently in the different Gospel traditions. (This is not the same as the older thesis that Jesus appeared many times to the Twelve, giving a different message each time, as now recorded in the various Gospels.) But an ever-increasing number of scholars doubt that the risen Jesus used words. Above (pp. 89–92) we discovered how difficult it was to understand the category of "seeing" applied to the appearances of the risen Jesus—the sight is not necessarily physical or available to all onlookers, and yet it is more than a purely internal experience. And so now we find that the category of "speaking" *may* be inadequate to describe the unique and eschatological encounter with the risen Jesus. The NT bears witness to the reality of a communication that took place during the appearance, and "speaking" seems to be the approximation in ordinary experience that best describes the extraordinary and indescribable.

Even if it seems that the various Gospel accounts of the appearances to the Twelve are variants of *one* appearance scene, by mentioning Jerusalem and Galilee the evangelists probably retain memories (vague, perhaps) of the movements of the Twelve after the death of Jesus. Let me offer the following *hypothesis* which has gained a certain favor among critical scholars. The basic appearance to the Twelve did not take place in Jerusalem on Easter Sunday—if it had taken place and they had been commissioned to a missionary endeavor, their subsequent return to their homes and occupations in Galilee would be difficult to explain. Rather, the Twelve fled Jerusalem and made their way back to Galilee, discouraged by the arrest and crucifixion of Jesus.[181] (We have yet to discuss the empty tomb;

---

[181] The exact moment of the flight of the Twelve from Jerusalem is not clear in the NT. One could interpret Mark 14:50 ("they all forsook him and fled") to mean a flight from Jerusalem at the time of Jesus' arrest. This is not the way Mark meant it, at least as regards Peter; for Mark and the other Gospels preserve a tradition that Peter was in Jerusalem during the interrogation of Jesus, at which time he denied Jesus. The Gospel witnesses that record an

but if we may anticipate from the next section, news that the body of Jesus was no longer in the tomb would only have increased the puzzlement and fright of the disciples, if they heard it before leaving Jerusalem.) As Simon Peter returned to his occupation of fishing, Jesus appeared to him on the shores of Sea of Tiberias[182] and resurrection faith was born. (Again, if we may anticipate, it would now have become clear why the tomb was empty: the Jesus whom Peter saw had been raised from the dead.) Subsequently Jesus appeared to the Twelve, confirming perhaps the inchoate faith stirred by Peter's report. It was on this occasion that the now glorified Lord poured forth his Spirit on those men and commissioned them to proclaim that the rule (kingdom) of God had been initiated on earth through what God had done for men in Jesus. As the Twelve would gradually discover, this general commission to proclaim the kingdom would involve bearing witness to Jesus in word and deed among all the nations, baptizing men and forgiving their sins, and bringing them into a community of the renewed Israel, a community that would ultimately be known as the Church. By the time of the development of the present Gospel narratives, all these specifications of the general commission had become evident and so they were incorporated verbally into the

---

appearance of the risen Jesus to the Twelve in Jerusalem on Easter Sunday night (Luke, John 20, and the Marcan Appendix) keep the Twelve on the scene for at least three days after the crucifixion; indeed, John 20:26 implies a period of over ten days. Perhaps even Mark 16:7 could be interpreted to support the presence of the Twelve in Jerusalem on Easter Sunday, if the directive to Magdalene and the women, "Tell his disciples and Peter that he is going before you to Galilee," means that the Twelve have not yet departed.

[182] In my commentary on John (n. 169 above), pp. 1085-95, I have suggested that the appearance in John 21:1-14 is composite and reflects two older traditions: one of an appearance at the lakeside to Peter the other of an appearance in Galilee to the Twelve at a meal. I contend that the former, preserved in John 21 in a mixed form, is the original *narrative* of what is cited in the formulas of I Cor 15:5 and Luke 24:34, namely, that the Lord appeared to Cephas or Simon. This appearance to Peter was Jesus' first post-resurrectional encounter with any member of the Twelve.

110 RAYMOND E. BROWN, S.S.

actual commission. The risen Jesus had led his Church to see what was mandated when he sent forth the Twelve.

It is difficult to be certain where this most important appearance to the Twelve took place. Galilee would seem the more likely site.[183] Why then would they have returned to Jerusalem? One possible explanation is that as observant Jews they went up to the holy city on the occasion of the next pilgrimage feast, namely, the Feast of Weeks or Pentecost.[184] In any case it was in Jerusalem on this feast that there took place a charismatic manifestation of the Spirit they had received from the risen Jesus. Catalyzed by this sign, the Twelve through Peter began to proclaim the good news that they perceived in faith: God had fulfilled His promises to Israel in Jesus whose crucifixion was not a defeat, for God had raised him and thus stamped his message and life with a seal of divine approval.

I have insisted that what I have offered in the last two paragraphs is a frequently accepted *hypothesis*. Whatever weaknesses it may have, it does more justice to the biblical data

---

[183] Critical scholars tend to favor Galilee because the thesis of an appearance to the Twelve at Jerusalem is usually associated with the thesis that Jesus appeared on Easter Sunday. However, there is little in the Gospel material critically considered to militate against the appearance to the Twelve having taken place in Jerusalem *after* Jesus had appeared to Peter in Galilee. One may object that, even if they are shorn of their chronology, the Lucan and Johannine accounts placing the appearance in Jerusalem are too theologically motivated to be dependable geographically. But the accounts that locate the appearance in Galilee are also theologically motivated. For instance, Matt 4:12-16 shows Matthew's interest in Galilee as the land of the Gentiles, and so the evangelist may have felt it fitting to locate in Galilee an appearance where Jesus commissions the Twelve to go and make disciples of all nations (28:19). As for the more specific Matthean localization of the appearance on "the mountain to which Jesus had directed them" (28:16), throughout the Gospel Matthew shows interest in a mountain that serves as the site of Christian revelation—a Christian Sinai, as it were (Matt 5:1; 14:23; 15:29; 17:1).

[184] C. F. D. Moule, "The Post-Resurrection Appearances in the Light of Festival Pilgrimages," *New Testament Studies* 4 (1957-58), 58-61.

critically examined than does the *equally hypothetical* harmonization of appearances that has Jesus begin to appear to the Twelve in Jerusalem on Easter and continue to appear to them when, for some inexplicable reason, they have gone to Galilee.

(C) Miscellaneous Considerations about the Appearances

Thus far I have concentrated on the sequence of the appearances of the risen Jesus because that is essential for understanding the problem of the empty tomb. But before I pass on to treat the empty tomb itself, let me note a few other considerations about the appearances that affect the discussion of bodily resurrection. (In part, this will involve gathering together observations already made in passing.)

Worthy of attention are the various ways in which the evangelists imply that the risen Jesus is no longer bound by the space-and-time laws of ordinary human experience. This is true even of Luke and John who, as we have seen, come closest to having a physical conception of the risen Jesus. Jesus is not recognized by Mary Magdalene (John 20:14), nor by the disciples on the road to Emmaus (Luke 24:16), nor by Peter and his fishing companions (John 21:4). One may get the impression that this lack of recognition is a failure on the part of Jesus' followers—Luke says, "Their eyes were kept from recognizing him"—but the Marcan Appendix 16:12 offers a different explanation: "He appeared in another form." This "otherness" of the risen Jesus is heightened by his ability to vanish (Luke 24:31) and reappear elsewhere (24:36), seemingly without traversing the space in between. John 20:19, 26 has Jesus appear in the middle of a room whose doors are shut.

If the risen Jesus seems to be free from the bonds of space, we can also see the evangelists wrestling with the problem of time. This comes to a head in a comparison of the Lucan, Johannine, and Matthean attempts to spell out the connection between resurrection and ascension. According to Luke, Jesus appeared before he ascended to heaven (Luke 24:51; Acts 1:9); and so the ascension terminated his visible presence (also the Marcan Appendix 16:19). According to the implications of John 20:17, Jesus appeared to Magdalene en route to his Father but appeared to his disciples after he had ascended. Yet although it was the ascended and glorified Jesus who appeared on Easter Sunday night and gave the Spirit to his disciples,[185] he did not remain visibly with his disciples; for Thomas was the last of those who saw the risen Jesus—all subsequent Christians will believe without seeing (20:29). According to Matthew, Jesus was exalted or glorified before he appeared to his disciples on the mountain in Galilee, for he claimed, "All authority in heaven and on earth has been given to me" (Matt 28:18). And there was no suggestion that he would depart again: "Behold, I am with you always, to the close of the age" (28:20). Indeed, some have questioned whether we should really consider Matt 28:16-20 as a post-resurrectional appearance narrative. It could be interpreted as the parousia of Jesus when he came back in glory to be with his disciples.[186]

If the various Gospel accounts thus betray the difficulty of framing the eschatological encounter with the risen Jesus in the categories of space and time, they also hint at the radically changed status of the one who appears. The post-resurrectional confession is not simply "We have seen Jesus" but "We have seen *the Lord*" (John 20:18, 25; 21:7; Luke 24:34). Since "Lord" is a christological evaluation of Jesus, the evangelists are telling us that the witnesses enjoyed not only *sight* of Jesus but also and even primarily *insight*. They saw that Jesus had been transferred into the realm of Lordship which is the realm of God. (See Acts 2:32, 36 which imply that through the res-

---

[185] John 7:39 says that there was no Spirit (given) during the ministry because Jesus had not yet been glorified. Thus the risen Jesus who gave the Holy Spirit in John 20:22 was a glorified Jesus.

[186] I am uncertain how far this should be pressed; for Matthew, writing some fifty years after the death of Jesus, certainly did not believe that the risen Jesus had been *visibly* present in the Christian community all that time. Perhaps we are to suppose that in the evangelist's lifetime it was common Christian knowledge that the appearances of the risen Jesus had been terminated, and so his abiding presence was of a different nature from what the Twelve had seen on a mountain in Galilee.

urrection Jesus was made Lord.) Thus, the appearances entail a sight that involves revelation, a sight that goes beyond ordinary experience.

IV. The Gospel Narratives
of the Empty Tomb

Before we can discuss the narratives themselves,[187] we must look at the Gospel information about the burial of Jesus, since the veracity of the story of the finding of the empty tomb presupposes the plausibility of the burial information.

(A) Details about the Burial of Jesus

Was Jesus buried in a recognizable tomb that could be visited by the women two days later? Many have pointed out that the normal procedure following the execution of an accursed criminal (Deut 21:23; Gal 3:13) would have been to dump the corpse into a common burial place reserved for malefactors. A few adventurous scholars have suggested that the very idea that the body of Jesus could not be found sprang from the impossibility of correctly identifying his body in such a common burial ground. However, an almost insuperable obstacle to such theorizing is raised by the person of Joseph of Arimathea who appears in all four Gospels.[188] It is virtually certain that he was not a figment of Christian imagination, that he was remembered precisely because he had a prominent role

---

[187] Helpful for this section is E. L. Bode, *The Gospel Account of the Women's Easter Visit to the Tomb of Jesus* (Rome: Angelicum, 1969).

[188] This may be less impressive than it seems; for in the main narrative of the empty tomb Matthew and Luke appear to be dependent on Mark, and only John (with whose tradition Luke agrees in part) seems to have an independent tradition. Thus we are dealing basically with only two traditions.

in the burial of Jesus, and thus that there was someone who knew exactly where Jesus had been buried.

Nor, if we approach the question from another angle, is it implausible that Jesus' body escaped the fate of burial in a common grave. Three of the Gospels (Matthew, Luke, and John) mention that Jesus' tomb was a new one, with Luke and John specifying that it was one "where no one had ever been buried." The latter detail may be an apologetic touch, similar to the apologetic motif we have found in Luke's and John's stress on the physical reality of the body of Jesus. But the "newness" of the tomb is neutral and may reflect an authentic memory that, although buried privately, the corpse of Jesus, accursed as it was under the Law, could still not be allowed to contaminate other corpses in a family grave. Since there was an element of hurry in the burial of Jesus, the choice of a hitherto unused tomb close to the place of execution (John 19:42) is quite plausible.

But would the Jewish authorities have allowed Jesus to be buried by his sympathizers? Acts 13:29 informs us that the *Jerusalem rulers* took Jesus down from "the tree" and laid him in a tomb. Some scholars maintain that this is a more authentic tradition than the Joseph of Arimathea story.[189] However, the Joseph story does make it clear that he was one of the rulers of the Jews (a member of the Sanhedrin). Thus the information could be reconciled if the Gospel accounts did not also present Joseph as a disciple of Jesus. We may speculate that he became a disciple later, and the introduction of his discipleship into the burial story was an anachronistic retrojection. At the time of

---

[189] There is also a scholarly attempt (e.g., Baldensperger) to combine the two ideas. Since John 19:31 reports that "the Jews" asked Pilate for the bodies of the crucified to be taken away and since John 19:38 reports that Joseph asked Pilate that he might take the body of Jesus away, a theory of two burials has been developed. It is proposed that the Jewish authorities buried Jesus in a common grave, but Joseph reburied him in a private grave, and that the idea of the empty tomb arose when those who did not know of the reburial visited the first grave. This theory is an indulgence in fantasy.

Jesus' death Joseph was probably no more than what Mark 15:43 makes him: "a respected member of the council who also looked for the kingdom of God,"[190] in short, a God-fearing man who extended to Jesus the burial that the Law commanded.

If we take the Joseph story as reflecting some historical tradition, there is still the problem of whether or not Jesus' body was anointed before burial. The suggestion that there was no proper burial preparation stems from the beginning of the empty tomb narratives in Mark 16 and Luke 24 where we are told that on the morning of the first day of the week Mary Magdalene and other women went to the tomb with spices[191] to anoint the body of Jesus. It is noteworthy that Matthew, who seemingly is dependent on Mark as regards the account of the empty tomb, changes drastically the stated purpose for the women's visit: they were going "to see the sepulcher," not to anoint the body. However, it is dubious that Matthew has corrected Mark on the basis of historical information. Matthew was trying to make the story of the visit to the tomb fit plausibly with the information that he (and he alone) recounted at the end of the burial scene, namely, that Pilate permitted the Jewish authorities to seal the tomb and to mount a guard of soldiers over it.[192] Obviously it would have been inconsistent for Matthew to report that

---

[190] If one compares the four Gospels, the character of Joseph grows with the telling. Not only has he become a disciple of Jesus in Matthew, but the tomb in which he buried Jesus was his own tomb (Matt 27:57, 60). Luke (23:50-51) stresses that he was a good and righteous man who had not consented to the action of the other members of the Sanhedrin in condemning Jesus (a contradiction of the "all" in Mark 14:64). John (19:39-40) has Joseph join Nicodemus in preparing Jesus' body for a solemn burial.

[191] The spices were prepared by the women immediately after the burial and before the Sabbath according to Luke 23:56. But according to Mark 16:1 the women bought the spices after Sabbath was passed! This disconcerting lack of agreement already raises a question about historicity.

[192] Most scholars regard the story of the guard as a Christian apologetic response to the contention that the body had been stolen. Benoit, p. 226, lists three serious objections against its historicity.

the women had set out with the hope of entering the tomb and having access to Jesus' corpse.

A greater contradiction stands between Mark/Luke and John. Not only does John not mention the women's purpose in coming to the tomb; but logically he excludes the possibility that the purpose was to anoint Jesus' body, for immediately after the crucifixion John has Joseph and Nicodemus join in preparing Jesus' body for burial, using an enormous amount of myrrh and aloes (one hundred pounds!—John 19:39-40). Once again there is doubt about John's historical exactitude because the main purpose of his burial narrative is symbolic.[193]

However, if there is hesitation about the reliability of the two accounts that exclude anointing as the purpose of the women's visit to the tomb, there is no certitude that Mark and Luke are historical in advocating this purpose. Several illogicisms have been detected in the Marcan/Lucan story, e.g., the oddity of seeking to anoint a body that had already corrupted for two days. I doubt the validity of such an objection since the evangelists knew the customs of the time and would scarcely have passed on what was manifestly unlikely. Perhaps the safe conclusion is to say that we cannot be sure whether Jesus' body was anointed before burial or not. (If it was anointed, then the women were probably going to the tomb to mourn.[194]) In any

---

[193] It illustrates the theme of John 12:32 that, once Jesus has been lifted up from the earth (in crucifixion), he begins to draw all men to himself. In John 19:38-39 two hitherto fearful men begin to confess publicly their adherence by preparing Jesus for burial. Moreover, the implausibly large outlay of spices may be meant to suggest that Jesus received a royal burial, thus continuing the theme of Jesus' kingship that is very strong in the Johannine Passion Narrative—see my commentary (n. 169 above), pp. 959-60.

[194] A custom of mourning for several days is implied by John 11:31, 39. For information on prolonged periods of mourning see A. Edersheim, *The Life and Times of Jesus the Messiah* (New York: Longmans, Green, 1897), I, 554-56; II, 316-20. The Midrash Rabba 100:7 on Gen 50:10 reports a rabbinic dispute on whether intense mourning could be cut down to two days and gives the opinion of Rabbi Bar Kappara (about A.D. 200) that mourning was at its height on the third day. Also see the Babylonian Talmud, *Semahoth* 8:1.

case, the reference to anointing with spices in Mark 16:1 and Luke 24:1 represents an editorial attempt to sew together more closely the story of the empty tomb and the main Passion Narrative.

(B) The Evolution of the Empty Tomb Narratives

Does this mean that the Passion Narrative once ended with the account of Jesus' burial and that an independent story about the finding of the empty tomb was added later? Some scholars answer negatively[195] because it is difficult to conceive of a basic Christian narrative that ended without an explicit assurance of Jesus' victory over death. This argument has value unless we are to theorize that belief in the risen Jesus was presupposed by those who narrated the passion, since a Passion Narrative would have no purpose unless Jesus had been victorious. The majority of scholars answer affirmatively,[196] and suggest that in Mark the two stories of burial and of empty tomb show signs of different origins. For instance, in Mark 15:47 we are told that Mary Magdalene and Mary the mother of Joses saw where Jesus was buried, but the names of the women who find the empty tomb (16:1) are Mary Magdalene, Mary the mother of James, and Salome. The names might be expected to agree if the narrative were consecutive.

If we agree to work with the hypothesis that the story of the

---

[195] U. Wilckens, "The Tradition-history of the Resurrection," in *The Significance of the Message of the Resurrection for Faith in Jesus Christ*, ed. by C. F. D. Moule (Studies in Biblical Theology, II #8; London: SCM, 1968), pp. 72-73, argues that the Passion Narrative once concluded with the story of the finding of the empty tomb but had no appearance narratives. W. Knox, *Sources of the Synoptic Gospels* (Cambridge University, 1953), I, 149, reconstructs a primitive Passion Narrative which contained a story wherein the women found the tomb empty and told the Twelve.

[196] The most complete study is that by L. Schenke, *Auferstehungsverkündigung und leeres Grab* (Stuttgarter Bibelstudien 33; Katholisches Bibelwerk, 1968). G. Schille, W. Nauck, and J. Kremer have also contributed to the discussion of this thesis.

THE VARIANT GOSPEL NARRATIVES OF THE VISIT OF THE WOMEN TO THE TOMB

	Mark 16:1–8	Matt 28	Luke 24	John 20
Time	Sabbath was past Very early First day of week Sun risen	Late on the Sabbath First day of week Growing light	First day of week At first dawn	Early First day of week Still dark
Women	Mary Magdalene Mary, mother of James Salome	Mary Magdalene Other Mary	Mary Magdalene Mary, mother of James Joanna Others	Mary Magdalene (Note "we" in vs. 2)
Purpose	Bought aromatic oils Came to anoint	Came to see tomb	Had aromatic oils from Friday Took aromatic oils along	
Visual Phenomena	Stone already rolled back Youth sitting inside on right	Earthquake Angel descended He rolled back the stone He sat on stone (outside)	Stone already rolled back Two men standing (inside)	Stone already moved away (Later) two angels sitting inside
Conversation	Youth said: Not to fear Jesus not here He is raised Tell disciples that he is going to Galilee There you will see him	Angel said: Not to fear Jesus not here He is raised Tell disciples that he is going to Galilee There you will see him	Men asked: Why seek living among dead? Jesus not here He is raised As he told you while still in Galilee	(Later) angels asked: Why do you weep? (Later) Mary answered: They took my Lord away (Later Jesus gives Mary a message for disciples)
Reaction	Women fled trembling, astonished Told no one	Women went away quickly with fear, great joy To tell disciples	Women left Told Eleven and rest	Mary ran to Peter and to Beloved Disciple Told them that body had been taken

finding of the empty tomb arose independently of the Passion Narrative, it is unlikely that Mark composed this story without incorporating older material, e.g., the second set of names above probably came to him already formed. The basic outlines of a pre-Marcan tomb story are suggested by the agreements in detail found in the accompanying chart. The reader will notice that in some details the Gospel witnesses to the story show very wide variance, especially as to the position and number of the angels.[197] But at least the following brief narrative might be distilled from agreements among the Synoptic accounts. On the first day of the week[198] Mary Magdalene and some other women went to the tomb of Jesus and found the stone rolled away from the entrance. A young man (or angel[199]) explained: "He is raised; he is not here." The women left the tomb fearful.

Schenke has strongly defended the thesis that this pre-

---

[197] The most notable example of how the narrative of the discovery of the empty tomb grew with the telling is Matthew's account. In Mark, Luke, and John the women find the stone already rolled back; but in Matt 28:2, after they have gone to the sepulcher, an earthquake takes place (an eschatological phenomenon that also accompanied the crucifixion according to Matt 27:51-52), and before their eyes "an angel of the Lord" descends from heaven and rolls back the stone. Matthew's tomb story is well on the way to becoming a description of the actual resurrection as happened in *The Gospel of Peter.*

[198] The other time specifications in the Gospels ("very early"; "sun risen"; "growing light"; "at first dawn"; "still dark") are confusing and even contradictory. They may represent two different versions: one, that the visit to the tomb took place just after sunset on the Sabbath (which, according to the lunar calendar, would already be the next day, the first of the week); the other, that it took place near dawn on Sunday morning. These two memories may be reflected in the difference between Mark's "When the Sabbath was passed" and Matthew's "Late on the Sabbath," unless Matthew's *opse sabbatōn* should be translated "after the Sabbath."

[199] Some scholars have taken the "young man" of Mark 16:5 as a human being and identified him with the young man of 14:51-52 who fled naked from Gethsemane when Jesus was arrested. For the arguments that he is meant to be an angel see Bode (n. 187 above), p. 27.

Marcan story reflects a cultic setting in the Jerusalem community as part of a ceremony of veneration at the tomb of Jesus. The time specification ("the first day of the week") indicated the day of cult; the message attributed to the angel was the solemn ceremonial explanation of the reason for veneration. We posited above that the early Christians would have known the whereabouts of Jesus' tomb; and in the first century the cult of venerating the tombs of holy men was well established in Palestine. Obviously, however, scholars cannot prove the existence of such a ceremony within a few years after Jesus' death.

In a paper originally given at the 1970 meeting on the resurrection at Rome (p. 14 above), J. Kremer[200] has made a different suggestion (that need not exclude all possibility of a cultic setting). He has concentrated on the function of the angelic appearances in the Gospel accounts of the discovery of the empty tomb and has compared them to similar appearances in Jewish apocalyptic literature where angels serve as interpreters of divine mysteries. These interpreting angels are often described as young men (cf. Mark 16:5); their appearance causes amazement (16:6) and fearful silence (16:8).

We may combine this suggestion with the observation of P. Benoit[201] that John 20:1-2, while undoubtedly Johannine in style, is the simplest of all the accounts of the visit to the empty tomb: Mary Magdalene (and perhaps companions—the "we" of verse 2) goes to the tomb on the first day of the week, finds the stone moved away, and leaves, thinking that the body of the Lord has been stolen. If we compare this Johannine account to the brief narrative distilled above from the Synoptic accounts, it differs only in not having an angel interpreter.[202] If the sub-

---

[200] "Die Überlieferung vom leeren Grab," in . . . *denn sie werden leben* (Stuttgart: Katholisches Bibelwerk, 1972), pp. 72-75.

[201] "Marie-Madeleine et les disciples au tombeau selon John 20, 1-18," in *Judentum, Urchristentum, Kirche* (n. 106 above), pp. 141-52.

[202] Angels appear on the scene in John 20:11-13, but these verses may represent another and more developed form of the empty tomb story, closer to the Synoptic accounts. See my commentary (n. 169 above), pp. 999-1000.

stance (as distinct from the wording) of the Johannine account constituted the original narrative about the empty tomb,[203] Kremer's theory would explain the introduction of the angels. The real explanation of why the tomb was empty would have become apparent only after Jesus had appeared to his disciples. The empty tomb and the appearances would have served mutually to enlighten one another: Jesus could appear because God had acted eschatologically and had raised him from the tomb, and the tomb was empty because Jesus was alive and had been taken to God. In order for Christians to develop a narrative of the empty tomb that they could pass on, they had to include the explanation as part of the story; and the way to do this was suggested by the patterns of apocalyptic literature, a literature that dealt with explaining God's eschatological mysteries. An angel or angels could be supplied to interpret the emptiness of the tomb, so that the story could now have a kerygmatic function. The bare historical fact that on the Sunday after his cruci-

---

[203] Doubt has been raised whether two of the items mentioned by John 20:1-2 would have been part of the original narrative. *First,* was the description of the rolled-back stone original, or was it first introduced when the narrative of the empty tomb was joined to the Passion Narrative in order to supply a connective? In Mark 15:46 and Matt 27:60 mention is made in the burial account of the placing of a stone at the door of the tomb, and so the connective theory is possible. (Almost certainly introduced as a connective was the dramatic touch of a debate about who would roll away the stone in Mark 16:3.) Yet the stone is not mentioned in the Lucan and Johannine burial accounts, so the connective theory is less applicable there, unless one wishes to claim that not only Luke but also John 20:1-2 has been influenced by Mark. Moreover, one may wonder whether later Christian reflection would have felt a compulsion toward having the tomb door stand open, since in our later accounts (Luke 24:36 and John 20:19, 26) the risen Jesus seems to be able to pass through obstacles. Thus, the bare fact of the stone being rolled away may be ancient. *Second,* was the suggestion that the body had been stolen part of the original narrative about the empty tomb? Or was it a later apologetic addition—an actual Jewish objection set into Mary Magdalene's mouth in order that it might be clearly refuted by what follows? I see no way to answer with certitude.

fixion Jesus' tomb was found empty could have been interpreted in many ways,[204] but it was woven into a narrative that became the vehicle of the basic Christian proclamation of Jesus' victory: *Jesus was raised.*[205]

To many Western readers the suggestion that an angelic appearance was "manufactured" to serve as an interpretation may seem outrageous rationalism, but that is because Christian readers of the Bible have understood too literally much of biblical angelology. What I have suggested has nothing to do with modern rationalism but flows from an attempt to understand properly the ancient Semitic mind. Many times in the OT when an "angel of the Lord" appears, this is simply a way of visibly describing God's speaking with men; and no separate angelic being is meant.[206] By the time of apocalyptic writing in the postexilic period (from the fifth century B.C. onwards), the idea of separate angelic beings had developed in Judaism, but even then most angelic interpreters were no more than mouthpieces for revelation, without any personality.[207] If we pay attention to the freedom with which the evangelists handled the details of the

---

[204] The idea that the story of the discovery of an empty tomb was invented for apologetic purposes runs against the objection that a mere empty tomb proves nothing about resurrection. Our earliest traces of Jewish apologetics against the resurrection do not reject the empty tomb; they explain that the body was taken away by the disciples or someone else. For instance, Tertullian, *De spectaculis* xxx (PL 1:662A) gives us the Jewish legend of the role of the gardener (see John 20:15): Jesus was buried in a vegetable garden, and the gardener removed the body because he did not want crowds coming to visit the tomb and trampling his cabbages. Moreover, were the story entirely an apologetic invention, *women* would not have been chosen as the ones to discover the tomb, since their testimony would have less public authority.

[205] R. H. Fuller, "The Resurrection of Jesus Christ," *Biblical Research* 4 (1960), 11-13.

[206] In Exodus 3:2 we are told that "the angel of the Lord" appeared to Moses in fire from the midst of the bush, but in 3:4 it is God Himself who speaks from the bush.

[207] The three "biblical" angels (Gabriel, Michael, and Raphael) have names terminating in "El" (= "God"), relating them very closely to divine activity, e.g., "Raphael" means "God has healed."

angelic appearance at the empty tomb (especially as to the number and position of the angels), we recognize their awareness that here they were not dealing with controllable historical facts but with imaginative description.[208]

Once the story of the finding of the empty tomb had become a vehicle of the proclamation of the resurrection, it was logical to join this story to the Passion Narrative. Indeed, the empty tomb story would ultimately become a bridge between the Passion Narrative and the narratives of the appearance of the risen Jesus. To facilitate relationship between the empty tomb story and the Passion Narrative such details were supplied as having the women come to the tomb to anoint the body of Jesus (Mark and Luke) or having them encounter the guards at the tomb (Matt 28:4). To facilitate relationship with the appended appearance narratives, the words of the interpreting angel(s) were expanded to include predictions or directives about future appearances. Mark's Gospel (if, as I suspect, there was no "lost ending") represents a stage in the development of the empty tomb story where, as yet, no appearance narratives have been appended, even though the reader is presumed to know of the appearances.[209] In the other three Gospels appearance narratives have been incorporated, and ultimately an unknown scribe brought Mark's Gospel into line by his addition of the Marcan Appendix which lists a series of appearances.

---

[208] Benoit, p. 260, remarks: "He [Mark] introduces an angel—a classical technique in the Bible—and puts the Easter kerygma into his mouth." Again, on p. 261: "When an author wanted to express a message from God, . . . it was an accepted custom to put it in the mouth of an angel." Actually, the angel was introduced into the basic narrative of the empty tomb not by Mark but in the pre-Marcan stage. The attempt to supply a kerygmatic proclamation cannot be dated so late as Mark himself, who otherwise shows little interest in angelic appearances.

[209] There is a growing consensus among scholars that Mark 16:7 (see also 14:28) was a redactional addition to the story of the empty tomb, intended to leave open the possibility of combining the tradition of the empty tomb with the tradition of appearances. There is less enthusiasm for the earlier suggestion of E. Lohmeyer that Mark was referring to a parousia to take place in Galilee.

Toward the beginning of this chapter we studied the pre-Pauline formula embodied in I Cor 15:3-5: "that Christ died . . . and that he was buried; that he was raised . . . and that he appeared." We found no clear proof that the formula's reference to *burial* implied the discovery of the empty tomb. In light of all that we have just seen, it would be more likely that, if there was an implicit reference to the empty tomb, it lies in the formula's statement "he was raised," especially if we include in the pre-Pauline formula the specification "on the third day." It is true that as I Cor 15:4 now stands, the resurrection itself is dated to the third day, but that may be a simplification. As we have noted, there is no other NT evidence that the early Christians tried to date exactly this eschatological event. What they did date was the discovery of the empty tomb on the first day of the week, which happened to be the third day after the burial. Since the empty tomb story became the setting and vehicle of the kerygmatic formula "Jesus was raised," it is not unlikely that the dating "on the third day" really reflects the events surrounding the empty tomb. A standard objection to this proposal is that the empty tomb story itself does not speak of the third day but of the first day of the week. However, the preservation of this reference to the first day of the week may have been dictated by cultic interests, as explained above. In other circumstances, when cultic usage was not involved, the dating "the third day" may have been preferred, either because of its possible relation to OT prophecy,[210] or because of its eschatological implications.[211] In summary, it is *possible* that "he was raised on the third day" implies the discovery of the

---

[210] Christians may well have seen in Hosea 6:2 ("On the third day he will raise us up") a reference to the resurrection, although our earliest evidence for a clear Christian citation of this passage is in Tertullian (*ca.* A.D. 210). We remember that Paul says that Jesus "was raised on the third day *according to the Scriptures.*"

[211] Fuller, pp. 25-27, drawing in part upon the evidence of the later Talmudic texts, points to the popular apocalyptic idea that the resurrection of the dead would occur three days after the end of the world.

empty tomb and the interpretation of that event by a faith engendered by the post-resurrectional appearances.[212]

V. Conclusions

With this return to our earliest evidence pertinent to the resurrection, i.e., the confessional formula, our discussion has come full circle. On pp. 108-111 above, I proposed a critical hypothesis explaining the sequence of events surrounding the post-resurrectional appearance of Jesus to the Twelve. Here I shall summarize the conclusions I would draw from all the evidence in the NT pertinent to the bodily resurrection of Jesus.

(1) The resurrection of Jesus, along with his exaltation and his giving of the Spirit, constituted an eschatological event—the beginning of the end-time. The categories of space and time, the categories of ordinary human experience such as "seeing" and "speaking" supply us with a language that is only analagous and approximate when we use it to describe the eschatological.[213] No one knows when the resurrection took place, for the NT writers can do no more than imply that it happened between the burial of Jesus and the discovery of the empty tomb. No one of them tries to describe it.

(2) The eschatological character of the resurrection has prompted some modern scholars to refuse to speak of the resurrection as historical. This is an unhappy development because the statement that the resurrection was not historical will be misinterpreted to mean that the resurrection never happened. Moreover, it probably does not do justice to the mystery of the

---

[212] See my caution in n. 142 above.

[213] Pope Paul VI alluded to this difficulty in conceptualizing in an important address on the resurrection delivered April 5, 1972 (text in the English edition of *L'Osservatore Romano,* April 13, 1972): "Jesus rose again in the same body he had taken from the Blessed Virgin, but in new conditions, vivified by a new and immortal animation, which imposes on Christ's flesh the laws and energies of the Spirit. . . . This new reality . . . is so far above our capacities of knowledge and even of imagination, that it is necessary to make room for it in our minds through faith."

resurrection; for, while the risen Jesus stood outside the bounds of space and time, by his appearances he touched the lives of men who were in space and time, men who were in history. The interaction of the eschatological and the historical should not be lost sight of.[214]

(3) The tomb of Jesus was not itself part of the eschatological event. Jesus was buried in a certain place. If that place was known, it could have been visited at a certain time. If the tomb was visited and it contained the corpse or skeleton of Jesus, it is difficult, if not impossible, to understand how the disciples could have preached that God raised Jesus from the dead, since there would have been irrefutable evidence that He had not done so.[215] It is therefore reasonably certain that either the tomb was not known, or that, if known, it was empty.

(4) The tradition that the tomb was known and was empty is considerably older than the Gospel narratives that have been built around the discovery of the empty tomb. It deserves preference[216] to the poorly supported hypothesis that the place of Jesus' burial was unknown. Of itself, the fact that the tomb was found empty allows several explanations. The idea that the body had been stolen may have been the first thought that occurred to Jesus' followers when they encountered the empty tomb.

(5) Of itself, then, the empty tomb was probably not at first a sign of the resurrection, and the emptiness of the tomb

---

[214] It was this interaction that Pope Paul pointed to in the same address when he spoke of the resurrection as "the unique and sensational event on which the whole of human history turns." This is not the same, however, as saying that the resurrection itself was a historical event, even though editorial writers quoted the Pope's speech to that effect. A perceptively nuanced discussion of this problem is found in P. Grelot, "L'historien devant la Résurrection du Christ," *Revue d'Histoire de la Spiritualité* 48 (1972), 221-50.

[215] This point is made persuasively by W. Pannenberg, "Did Jesus Really Rise from the Dead?" *Dialog* 4 (1965), 18-35.

[216] This tradition has been judged historical by one of the most critically adept contemporary Church historians, namely H. von Campenhausen, "The Events of Easter and the Empty Tomb," *Tradition and Life in the Church* (Philadelphia: Fortress, 1968), pp. 42-89.

was not formally a part of Christian faith in the risen Jesus. Modern fundamentalist statements such as "Our faith depends on the empty tomb" or "We believe in the empty tomb" are not only open to ridicule about the emptiness of one's faith, but also misplace the emphasis in resurrection faith. Christians believe in Jesus, not in a tomb.

(6) In the genesis of resurrection faith it was the appearance of the glorified Lord that first brought his disciples to believe; and this belief, in turn, interpreted the empty tomb. Having seen the risen Jesus, they understood that the reason why the tomb was empty was because he had been raised from the dead. Thus Christians confessed a Jesus who both *was raised* and appeared (I Cor 15:4-5; Luke 24:34). Consequently, while the empty tomb was not an object of Christian faith, it was not unrelated to that faith, for it colored the way in which the faith was proclaimed.

(7) Ultimately the insight of faith shaped the *narratives* of the discovery of the tomb. The revealed solution to the ambiguity of the empty tomb, namely, that it was empty because Jesus had been raised, was incorporated into these narratives by the introduction of one or more angels who proclaimed: "He was raised" (Mark 16:6).

(8) In the other direction, the idea of the empty tomb had an effect on the *narratives* of the post-resurrectional appearances of Jesus. The fact that the tomb was discovered empty on the first day of the week affected the dating and location attached by Luke and John to the appearance of Jesus to the Twelve (on the same day in Jerusalem). The tomb supplied an important element in the continuity between the career of the earthly Jesus and that of the risen Jesus, so that there was a tendency to take the language appropriate to one career and apply it to the other career, e.g., body, see, touch.

And so from a critical study of the biblical evidence I would judge that Christians can and indeed should continue to speak of a *bodily* resurrection of Jesus. Our earliest ancestors in the faith proclaimed a bodily resurrection in the sense that they did not think that Jesus' body had corrupted in the tomb. However, and this is equally important, Jesus' risen body was no longer a body as we know bodies, bound by the dimensions of space and time. It is best to follow Paul's description of risen bodies as spiritual, not natural or physical (*psychikos*—n. 147 above); he can even imply that these bodies are no longer flesh and blood (15:50). Small wonder that he speaks of a mystery! In our fidelity to proclaiming the bodily resurrection of Jesus, we should never become so defensively governed by apologetics that we do not do justice to this element of transformation and mystery. Christian truth is best served when equal justice is done to the element of continuity implied in bodily resurrection and to the element of eschatological transformation.

The understanding that the resurrection was bodily in the sense that Jesus' body did not corrupt in a tomb has important theological implications. The resurrection of Jesus was remembered with such emphasis in the Church because it explained what God had done *for men*. Through the resurrection men came to believe in God in a new way; mankind's relationship to God was changed; a whole new vision of God and His intention for men was made possible; the whole flow of time and history was redirected. Nevertheless, a stress on the *bodily* resurrection keeps us from defining this resurrection solely in terms of what God has done for men. The resurrection was and remains, first of all, what God has done *for Jesus*. It was not an evolution in human consciousness, nor was it the disciples' brilliant insight into the meaning of the crucifixion—it was the sovereign action of God glorifying Jesus of Nazareth. Only because God has done this for His Son are new possibilities opened for His many children who have come to believe in what He has done.

The fact that these future possibilities for Christians *are* patterned on what God has already done for Jesus lends a special importance to the question of bodily resurrection. In man's anticipation of God's ultimate plan, one of two models is usually followed: the model of eventual destruction and new creation, or the model of transformation. Will the material world pass away and all be made anew, or will somehow the world be transformed and changed into the city of God? The model that the Christian chooses will have an effect on his attitude toward the world and toward the corporeal. What will be destroyed can have only a passing value; what is to be transformed retains its importance. Is the body a shell that one sheds, or it is an intrinsic part of the personality that will forever identify a man? If Jesus' body corrupted in the tomb so that his victory over death did not involve bodily resurrection, then the model of destruction and new creation is indicated. If Jesus rose bodily from the dead, then the Christian model should be one of transformation. The problem of the bodily resurrection is not just an example of Christian curiosity; it is related to a major theme in theology: God's ultimate purpose in creating.

EPILOGUE

The problems discussed in this book are problems that must be faced and discussed by all Christians. If they have become of particular urgency to Roman Catholics, it is because of the conjunction of two factors in the post-Vatican II Church. First, the Church has now officially encouraged and accepted the methods of modern biblical criticism; and this criticism especially affects former understandings of the infancy narratives and the post-resurrectional narratives as eyewitness history. Second, there is an increasing appreciation that past formulations of dogma are conditioned in their phrasing by time and circumstances, so that, while they catch an aspect of the truth, they do not exhaust it. Following Pope John's distinction between the deposit of faith and the way in which it is presented, Catholic theologians are maintaining the sometimes older formulations have to be modified by more recent insights. Obvious candidates for serious restudy are doctrines whose basis would be affected by modern critical studies of the Bible, such as the virginal conception and the bodily resurrection.

My purpose in the book has been modest: not to give doctrinal answers as if biblical criticism were the ultimate court of appeal, but to survey the evidence as objectively as possible to see what biblical scholarship might contribute to the Church's discussion of these doctrines. I know that some Catholic writers, often on a popular level, have already pronounced that biblical criticism has so eroded the basis of the traditional formulations about the virginal conception and the bodily resurrection that these formulations should be abandoned. That is *not* the conclusion that I would reach.

131

I have found that the biblical evidence, even when re-evaluated by current scientific methods, continues to favor the idea of a bodily resurrection, although at the same time it serves to correct a notion popular in the past that would equate resurrection with physical resuscitation. The eschatological context of the bodily resurrection and the analagous character of the language used to describe the risen Jesus are clearer today than previously.

Nor do I think that modern biblical study favors abandoning the idea of a virginal conception, although the situation here is more ambiguous because of the very limited NT evidence and the need of more examination in the context of ecumenical scholarship. Scripturally I judge that it is harder to explain the tradition about the virginal conception by positing theological creation than by positing fact. But more work should be done to see how the "high" explicit christology of the accounts of the virginal conception can be reconciled with the lower implicit christology that, by the common consent of scholars Catholic and Protestant, marked the ministry of Jesus. Moreover, it should be clarified for Catholics that the doctrines of the sanctity of Mary and of the incarnation of God's Son are not logically dependent on the virginal conception. Also the tendency should be resisted to cite the creeds simplistically as an answer to the problem of the virginal conception, since the basic focus of the article "born of the Virgin Mary" seems to have been the *birth* of God's Son from a truly human parent (thus his undeniable humanity—flesh of flesh), rather than a definition of the biological manner of his *conception*. The custom of speaking of virgin birth rather than virginal conception complicates the discussion at hand.

The relatively conservative conclusions I have drawn from the evidence, conclusions *favoring* the retention of the traditional formulations of virginal conception and bodily resurrection, will disappoint some Catholic liberals who may even wonder whether I studied the evidence without doctrinal predetermination. In our polarized Church the accusation of currying favor with the authorities is quickly hurled at those who affirm traditional formulations. On the other side of the spectrum, my desire to approach the biblical evidence without assuming that the conclusions have been dictated by past doctrines will annoy that extreme within Catholicism which sees no human or modifiable element in the formulations of the past and which categorizes as arrogant heresy any attempt to study the problems anew, unless that attempt has as its purpose finding more arguments to bolster what the Church has already said. Critics of this mind will also reject as equivocation all shading that a critical biblical study brings to the understanding of past formulations, even if that study basically supports the retention of the formulations. The answer to the first group of liberal critics is to insist on the integrity and responsibility of biblical criticism; the answer to the second group of fundamentalist critics is to insist on the rights of biblical criticism. But biblical criticism, despite its sponsorship by recent Popes, is too new on the Catholic scene for either its responsibility or its rights to be respected by all. Only when this respect is accorded, can biblical scholars loyal to the teaching authority of the Church make their special contribution to the larger picture of Catholic thought.

INDEX OF AUTHORS

(This is primarily an index that lists the *first* occurrence of a modern author's book or article.)